Who has Spoken b[barcode obscures text]

GW00420338

As Christians we tend to think (preparation for Christ, and foretelling the coming of Chris these beliefs. But we miss a significant part of the Old Testament, and specifically of the prophets, if we do not realise that for the Jews the Old Testament remains their Scriptures, which have sustained them through centuries of homelessness, persecution and oppression. Today the Law and the Prophets are the main elements in synagogue worship. A young man in a synagogue in London, Manchester or Leeds, for instance, could read the passage from Isaiah which Jesus read to the people in the synagogue at Nazareth (Luke 4). It would have a meaning for the Jewish worshippers quite separate from what we, as Christians, derive from it.

These studies attempt to penetrate the original significance of the messages of the prophets as well as to link them to the Christian gospel where appropriate. We shall ask whether the original message can still be relevant to us in our age, and how far understanding the prophets may also help us to understand Jesus.

Here modern translations are of great help. Both James Moffat's translation and the New English Bible are excellent for bringing out the meaning of obscure passages and words. For the first four studies also J. B. Phillips has an outstanding translation entitled *Four Prophets*.

I have added questions to each chapter and one or two activities for the group which I hope will be useful. These questions give the reader a guide in 'doing their homework' before the group meeting and may help the leader to shape the discussion.

I hope you enjoy your study.

Frank Collier
November 2001

CONTENTS

Introduction

Some preliminary information about the prophets

The Old Testament prophets lived and preached during a period of 400 years between 770 BC and 350 BC. Generally these were times of crisis.

It had not always been so. Just before 1000 BC David became king of Israel and he and his son Solomon after him created a wealthy and powerful kingdom. After Solomon's death, however, the country split into two, much as some Balkan countries have done in recent years. The northern part became the kingdom of Israel with its capital at Samaria. The southern part became the kingdom of Judah with its capital at Jerusalem. Unhappily the two constantly quarrelled and in doing so lost any capacity to defend themselves effectively against Egypt and the very aggressive Assyrians.

It was in those days that the first of the prophets appeared, and you will notice that on top of the usual hazards of famine, locusts, cattle disease and pestilence, there are constant references to war and bloodshed.

After 800 BC the situation worsened and Israel, the northern kingdom, was in serious danger. It is at this time that *Amos* and *Hosea* pleaded with Israel to repent in order that God might save them from disaster. Their pleas went unheeded and in 721 BC the Assyrians conquered Israel and took its better-off people into exile as slaves.

Judah survived until 586 BC. At first the Assyrians were a threat to Jerusalem and it was at this time that *Isaiah of Jerusalem* (author of most of Isaiah 1-39) and *Micah* were active as prophets. However, it was not the Assyrians but the more powerful Chaldeans under Nebuchadnezzar who conquered Jerusalem. The prophet *Jeremiah* was

1

preaching in the years just before 586 BC and immediately afterwards. The better-off people of Judah were taken to Babylon in the same way that the northern Israelites had been taken to Assyria. During the Exile of the people of Judah in Babylon, there arose a *second Isaiah* whose work we can read in Isaiah 40-55.

It is important to be clear in our minds just what the prophets were. They were not religious clairvoyants. They were men morally sensitive to the evil and injustice around them and to the disloyalty of their nation to God. Their messages were often warnings to the people about the calamitous consequences of persistent wrongdoing. Yet all but one of them, Amos, could speak hopefully of God's forgiveness if they would but repent.

Inevitably they were often rather lonely figures. Jeremiah, for instance, was imprisoned for treason, and one unnamed prophet may have been put to death (Isaiah 53). Their preaching was simple. They used everyday images and relationships to convey their message – potters' wheels, plumb lines, baskets of fruit, and the metaphor of marriage.

What is important for us is the high and often severe claim which they made upon God's people. That is unchanging and timeless.

Chapter 1

Hosea and the God of Israel

Halts by me that footfall:
Is my gloom, after all,
Shade of his hand, outstretched caressingly?
'Ah, fondest, blindest, weakest,
I am he whom thou seekest!
Thou dravest love from thee, who dravest me.'

Francis Thompson
'The Hound of Heaven'

Passages for study: Hosea 1, 2, 3, 4, 6:4-9, chapters 11 and 12.

The significance of Hosea

Nowhere in the Old Testament, save perhaps in the writings of the second Isaiah, are the great themes of the Old Testament, and especially of the Old Testament prophets, so clearly seen as in the prophecy of Hosea. We saw in the Introduction that he lived just before the destruction of the northern kingdom by the Assyrians. He brought into focus all that Israel had learned of God, and yet struck a characteristically personal note which prepared the way for Jeremiah and the second Isaiah. So it is appropriate that we should let him set the stage for our studies of the prophets.

A personal dilemma

Unlike Amos, who also warned the northern people of imminent disaster, Hosea was a native of the northern kingdom and he loved his people. Like Jesus lamenting over Jerusalem, Hosea could not hide the anguish which he suffered because he was compelled to warn Israel of impending catastrophe. I am reminded of a young

German, Adam van Trott, who was among those executed in 1945 for the attempted assassination of Hitler. He had many friends in Britain who all knew that Adam hated Hitler and all his works. But they could not understand why he could not bear to hear them violently criticising Germany. He loved Germany and inwardly suffered anguish because of its crimes. Hosea would have understood how he felt.

Hosea faces a more intimate dilemma too. In Hosea 1:2 God tells Hosea to marry a woman who will be unfaithful to him. He does so (v3). Three children are born of the marriage, and as often happens in the Old Testament they are given symbolic names. The first is Jezreel as a sign that God will punish the kings of Israel for sins committed at Jezreel. The other two are named Unloved (v6) and Stranger (v9), suggesting that Israel is unloved and a stranger to God.

Scholars disagree as to whether Hosea actually married a woman of loose moral habits. My own feeling is that the passionate intensity and pleading of this prophecy is the fruit of a deeply disturbing experience from which Hosea has derived a remarkable insight. He sees that just as he finds it impossible to cease to love his unfaithful wife, so God cannot cease to love the disobedient and unfaithful Israel.

This is made very clear in the succeeding chapters. The dark forebodings concerning Israel's future are interspersed with a persistent faith in the power of God's love.

Chapter 2 compares Hosea's own personal anguish to the anguish of God. First there is anger and the warning of terrible punishment for Israel. The people have worshipped idols as if they have provided them with prosperity (v5) when it was God who was their benefactor (v8). Famine and poverty are threatened (v9-10) and Israel will pay for her idolatry (v11-13). Then there follows a 'wooing' of Israel (v14-15) and a promise that the people will be freed from the service of idols (v16-17). Once more Israel will be united with her God (v19-23).

The optimism seems short-lived, however, and in chapter 3 Hosea faces again the unfaithfulness of his wife. By comparison he realises that the rehabilitation of Israel may be a long and painful process. The hardship which Hosea had hoped would cleanse Israel had not done so and, as so often happens in history, it had simply been followed by a return to loose living once more – much in the way that the debauchery of the reign of Charles II followed the austerity and rigour of the time of Cromwell.

Hosea's inheritance

The central faith of the Old Testament is that God is active in the life of his people, and this is also the central theme of the prophecy.

It is God who is the initiator. The prophecy begins with the word of God coming to Hosea and this divine initiative is repeated four times in chapter 1 alone. Equally when God speaks of his relationship with Israel, as, for instance, at the beginning of chapter 11, it is God who loves Israel and calls her into a very special relationship. This can be seen in earlier Old Testament writings and reminds us of the call of Abraham and Moses.

If we forget that everything originates in God's purpose we shall not only fail to understand the prophets, but the Old Testament as a whole.

Equally we must never lose sight of the close relationship with God which Hosea emphasises throughout the prophecy. This is particularly noticeable in chapters 11 and 12. Hosea describes God leading the people of Israel and teaching them as a parent teaches a child, even the simplest movements like walking (11:3). There is the parental comfort for the stumbling child and the encouragement that most children need (11:3-4), and this metaphor is used to depict God's dealing with Israel.

In chapter 12 the prophet shows God appealing to Israel's memory of his faithfulness to them throughout their history.

He reminds them of the faith and spiritual stamina of Jacob (12:2-5). Verse 6 contains an appeal for Israel to return to God and to put its trust in him. The appeal is continued as God points out that it is he who inspires the prophets, just as he had inspired the prophet Moses to lead Israel out of Egypt.

This emphasis on history is very typical of Judaism. It has also been handed down to the Christian Church because it is in a historic event, the life, the death and resurrection of Jesus, that the Christian faith is founded. And just as the great festivals of the Jewish faith are centred in historic events like the deliverance from Egypt in the Passover, and the giving of the Law at Pentecost, so our sacrament is rooted in the historic death of Jesus.

The originality of Hosea
Earlier prophets like Elijah and Elisha had called for exclusive obedience from Israel to God. They too had condemned idolatry as Hosea does.

But Hosea connects idolatry and the abandonment of true faith with the moral behaviour of the people:

> There is no faithfulness or loyalty, and no knowledge of God in the land . . . bloodshed follows bloodshed. Therefore the land mourns, and all who lie in it languish.
>
> Hosea 4:1-3

For this he blames the prophets and priests who have led them astray (4:4-11). They are accused of changing a glorious calling into a shameful trade. 'They feed on the sin of my people; they are greedy for their iniquity' (v8).

As a result the people are dying for lack of spiritual knowledge (4:6). So they worship God but have no knowledge of what he requires of them. One is reminded of some words of John Wesley:

> When you speak to God, do your lips and heart go together? Do you often utter words by which you mean just nothing?

Hosea is also aware that material prosperity has been ruinous to Israel's spiritual life. This is graphically expressed in chapter 12:7f:

> Swindler! He loves to cheat
> With false balances in his hand.
> And does Ephraim say, Yes, but I have grown rich,
> I have made myself wealthy?
> All his gains can never outweigh
> The guilt that he has amassed.

In chapter 6:6 Hosea gathers all this together in what is perhaps the most familiar line in the prophecy:

> For I desire steadfast love and not sacrifice,
> the knowledge of God rather than burnt
> offerings.

This shows how Hosea was already realising that the spiritual malady of his people was deeply rooted and that the true sign of unreserved obedience to God lay in a radically changed moral attitude. That was a first important step which Judaism and the Christian faith owe to Hosea and his contemporary prophets. It is no accident that Jesus himself quoted these words in Matthew 9:13.

The second step forward is rather less obvious. It is difficult for men and women in such a highly individualistic age as our own to enter into the way that the people of the Old Testament thought.

Their relationship with God was not an individual one. They were part of the people of God and they worshipped as a people. Their righteousness was established by their fulfilment of their obligations to their community. If God prospered Israel, they shared the prosperity, whether they deserved it or not. If God chastised Israel, they shared in the calamity, whether they were innocent or guilty.

Nowhere in the prophecy does Hosea suggest that God differentiates between those who forsake him and those who continue to be faithful. But his own agonised consciousness of the nearness of God to him and his inner certainty that God had spoken to him (1:1-5 and 12:10-14) lifts him into a position of isolation from his people and must have made him aware of a personal communion with God. This was not entirely new because Moses had enjoyed such communion, and Elijah had certainly been conscious of isolation and of his communion with God. But Hosea expresses his personal faith perhaps more sharply.

Anyone reading only chapter 11 would feel the contrast between the anger and the love of God which are there depicted. But it is an anger born of love, much like the anger of a mother who discovers her boy unharmed after some mischievous but dangerous escapade, and scolds him before tearfully embracing him with her sheltering arms. The picture Hosea gives us is a very human representation of the divine love. And that love is always in the ascendant. Perhaps nowhere in the Old Testament is there such a vivid portrayal of the love which one day would be seen in the face of Jesus.

Some reflections

The prophets of the eighth century BC are often described as the prophets of ethical monotheism ie. prophets who proclaimed that there was one God over all who demanded from his people not ritual sacrifices, but moral obedience. This was true of Amos, Isaiah and Micah as well as Hosea. What characterises Hosea and Amos particularly, however, is the insight that moral decadence seems to be connected to affluence, that wealth and riches divert the attention of men and women from the essential discipline of moral obedience to God towards an obsession with material comfort and display, and indirectly to cutting moral corners to satisfy those greedy desires. In my view the prophecy therefore asks the same questions of our own age as it did of eighth-century Israel. What do you think?

The ageless conflict in our thinking of God is mirrored here too. We find it hard to strike the right balance between the concern of God for righteousness and his merciful readiness to forgive and restore us. Attempts to resolve the issue too often end in a rather artificial severing of the being of God into two opposite persons – an angry and stern Father and a merciful Son. Hosea's understanding of human parental love and the way in which firmness and even anger can sometimes express that love, does help us to recognise how God's love can express itself for us.

Finally Hosea shows us how our own experience of the preciousness of human love, its joys, its anguish, its anxieties and its capacity for endurance do tell us something about God. We shall see in our studies of the second Isaiah how this developed. But best of all we shall find that it is in the love of Jesus, in all its human aspects and possibilities, that we can see for ourselves the love that God revealed to Hosea through his own suffering amidst a faithless people.

Questions

1. Hosea learned from the experience of suffering. What kind of lessons about God can we learn from adversity, from bitter disappointment, from physical suffering, and even from our sins?

2. Weigh the evidence for the view that hardship and adversity will bring men and women back to God.

3. Look at Hosea 2:16-18 and 14:5-7. These passages appear to suggest that when Israel is restored to God's favour there will be material prosperity. Does forgiveness necessarily mean that we shall have material comfort or that life will be easier?

4. By contrast, do you accept the view that affluent societies nearly always become morally decadent? If so, why?

5. Look at some of the following passages: Matthew 9:36; Luke 15; Luke 19:41-42. In what ways are the words of Jesus similar to those of Hosea in what they say of God?

6. Collect some hymns which speak of the suffering love of God. How much do they owe to an understanding of suffering human love?

7. Henry McKeating speaks of the God of Israel as an 'active God'. Look at the prophecy and list some ways in which that activity expresses itself. What do you learn from your study?

8. If a member of your group has access to one of the poems below, see if you can find points at which there is an echo of Hosea: John Masefield, 'The Everlasting Mercy'; Francis Thompson, 'The Hound of Heaven'; John Milton, *Paradise Regained*. If you are spending more than one session on this chapter, you could have one or two brief readings.

Chapter 2

Amos, Prophet of the Judgement of God

> Prophecy is a function of the Church, and must be so till the end of time, for it will always be the duty of the Church to proclaim that this world is God's world, and that infringements of his law will bring their own terrible penalties. Sin is not and never can be a purely personal matter. The problem of evil affects the whole human race.
>
> Trevor Huddleston, *Naught for Your Comfort*

Passages for study: Amos 1, 2, 3:1-8, 5:6-24, 7:7-17.

Judgement and the Christian Gospel

The words of Archbishop Huddleston, whose work involved him in proclaiming judgement on an unjust society, have much in common with those of the prophet Amos, who was a prophet of judgement.

Today the theme of judgement only rarely appears in Christian sermons, but this is a relatively new phenomenon. Visit the parish church of the Cotswold town of Fairford. There you will find stained glass windows beginning at the north-west corner and telling the whole biblical story. The great west window depicts the Day of Judgement. Imagine a rural congregation in other days turning to leave the church after worship to be faced by that inescapable warning of the judgement to come. Or imagine a congregation in a Methodist church two centuries ago, as they listened to similar warnings from the pulpit. Sometimes the element of love and compassion appeared to be absent and fear was the dominant element. It was very different from the atmosphere of churches today.

To understand Amos it is necessary to recover that atmosphere of impending judgement, which was once as much part of Christian worship as it is here in the Old Testament.

Who was Amos?

He was active about 30 years before Hosea. It is fairly obvious that conditions in the Northern Kingdom were little different from those which Hosea describes. People worshipped foreign gods, possibly with the sacrifice of children. Evil religious practices went hand in hand with moral decadence.

Amos was not a native of the Northern Kingdom but came from Judea. He was a shepherd and tended sycamore trees (7:14). Though a foreigner he was a 'relative' much like a Welshman is a relative of the Celtic Scots and Irish. In one way this was an advantage because it is not always easy to address words of warning and judgement to one's own people, and friends and family.

To the sophisticated town dwellers of the north he doubtless appeared like a country bumpkin, with his dress, his uncouth speech, and his wild words. People may have thought him mad or at best a fanatic. J. B. Phillips has likened him to a stern and relentless Calvinist preacher from the Scottish highlands descending on a prosperous British city today.

Perhaps the resentment experienced by Archbishop Huddleston in South Africa was not dissimilar, because as a foreigner he was regarded as impertinent in condemning apartheid.

Amos was not a professional prophet (7:14). He was not a prophet's son; he did not prophesy for fees but relied on his strong conviction that God had called him.

The prospect of judgement

From very early days the Hebrews had looked forward to the Day of the Lord when they hoped that God would put an end to their suffering, punish their enemies and give them a material paradise.

Amos stands that idea firmly on its head. He begins with a series of judgements against the surrounding peoples. Notice that the evils are what we today would call social or national evils. Damascus is condemned for outrages against her neighbours, the Philistines because they have enslaved whole populations, and Tyre because its rulers have sold whole tribes into slavery (1:3-10). The Edomites are condemned for fratricide and the people of Ammon for outrages against pregnant women (1:11-15). Finally Amos pronounces judgement against his own people in Judah because of their idolatry (2:4-5).

Up to that moment doubtless he would have had an enthusiastic hearing from the Israelites who would relish the discomfiture of their enemies. But then the lash descends on them (2:6-8). A handful of silver has secured perjured evidence against the innocent (v6). People in debt have been sold into slavery and the proceeds used to buy an expensive pair of shoes (v6). They are accused of grinding the poor and exploiting the weak. Men defile themselves with temple prostitutes (v7). Their very furnishings are the pledges they took for what turned out to be bad debts and the judges are so corrupt that they buy their wine with the exorbitant fines which they have imposed (v8). Israel's behaviour has been as outrageous as that of her enemies.

Like Hosea, Amos reminds the Israelites of all that God has done for them, concentrating on the deliverance from slavery in Egypt and the settlement of the tribes in Canaan. (2:9-11). Then there follows a description of the punishment which is to follow (2:13-16). No one will escape, not even the strongest, the fastest runner or the most accomplished horseman. As he says in 5:20:

> Is not the day of the Lord
> darkness, not light,
> and gloom with no brightness in it?

The criterion of judgement

In chapter 5 Amos analyses further the nature of Israel's disobedience.

First he condemns them because they have no regard for human dignity:

> Therefore because you trample on the poor and take from them levies of grain, you have built houses of hewn stone, but you shall not live in them.
>
> (5:11)

He condemns them for perverting God's justice. For him justice is not a matter of human convenience:

> They hate the one who reproves in the gate, and they abhor the one who speaks the truth.
>
> (5:10)

> For I know how many are your transgressions, and how great are your sins – you who afflict the righteous, who take a bribe, and push aside the needy in the gate.
>
> (5:12)

They are God's people perverting God's justice.

He condemns them because there is such a contrast between the luxury of the rich and the desperate needs of the poor.

> Alas for those who lie on beds of ivory, and lounge on their couches, and eat lambs from the flock, and calves from the stall; who sing idle songs to the sound of the harp, and like David improvise on instruments of music; who drink wine from bowls, and anoint themselves with the finest oils, but are not grieved over the ruin of Joseph!
>
> 6:4f

The name Joseph is used as a synonym for the poor people of Israel.

In chapter 5:21f he links these social sins to their false worship. God does not want their noisy worship:

> But let justice roll down like waters,
> And righteousness like an everflowing stream.

In a word, bad religion causes bad morality and moral failure leads to religious idolatry.

It is easy to stand back and recognise the evil which Amos exposes without recognising that the people of Israel may well have been good parents, anxious for the welfare of their families and eager to provide for them. They may have been loyal friends in their own circle. They may have had strong convictions about loyalty to the nation. Privately they may have been likeable, just as those men and women often are today who by their social selfishness and pursuit of material wealth injure the poor and unfortunate.

Sometimes, then as now, this happened because of ignorance. It is so easy to make snap judgements about people whose needs and difficulties we do not understand. Sometimes, too, our spiritual insecurity will make us try to obtain a material security at whatever cost to our fellows. Doubtless Amos encountered people like ourselves.

The implications of judgement

Anyone coming fresh to Amos will be appalled by the long list of catastrophes which Amos says are God's punishment of Israel. Pointedly in chapter 3:6 he says 'Does disaster befall a city unless the Lord has done it?' This, of course, is typical of peoples who assume that suffering is a sign of divine anger. This is not a Christian viewpoint. We may question the wisdom of people who live in San Francisco so near to the San Andreas fault, but we should never ascribe the disaster of earthquake to the hand of God. Here the New Testament questions the Old.

But Amos still has something to say to us. Look at the picture of the plumb-line in Amos 7:7-9. There God is pictured testing the uprightness of a wall with the aid of a plumb-line. This is not a wilful capricious judgement. The plumb-line appeals to the law of gravity. It does not rely on the feelings of the builder. By comparison the judgement of God is not that of divine anger, but the inevitable working out of laws which God respects as much as man must do.

If we apply that principle we shall see that just as the natural world has its laws, so does God's moral universe. Fire burns. Floods drown. Gravity is universal. Whether we are good or bad, Christians or agnostics, we are all subject to those laws. So also there is a moral context which we cannot defy with impunity.

For instance, deep-seated hatreds have been known to destroy the physical and mental health of men and women. So, even more obviously, have addictions to drink and drugs and sexual immorality.

We may find forgiveness both human and divine, but that may not prevent us from carrying the scars of misdoing, and we have to accept the penalties which ensue when we defy God's moral universe. Deeds have consequences.

Some years ago I was visiting a hospital when there was a power cut and nurses were rushing around providing alternative lights. 'What must it have been like before electricity?' said one. I pointed out that part of the problem was that the hospital worked by electricity, and when that failed crisis ensued. Perhaps it is true that God means his universe to work by love and justice, and when that fails, it will not work in any other way. Deeds have consequences.

It would be wrong, however, to stop short of the gospel. Henry McKeating has rightly said:

> What Amos offers us is something less than a gospel. He can speak with the tongues of men and of angels, and his faith is second to none other's. But he offers no hope, and perhaps, in the end, little love either . . . The least preacher of Christ will take precedence over him.

There is much to ponder here.

Some reflections

Hidden away in the prophecy is an assumption made by Elijah, and perhaps by Hosea too, that rural life, or the life of the desert and the wilderness, was morally healthier than the life of cities. Is this true? A modern political philosopher, the American Herbert Marcuse, has argued that much of the violence of modern life is rooted in urban living. He might be surprised to think that he was echoing the words of Hebrew prophets.

Amos also makes the assumption that all life belongs to God and that as God's messenger he must speak about every aspect of human life. Until the Reformation that was also the assumption of the Christian preacher. In the 16th century Bishop Hugh Latimer attacked the policies of the Crown and tore into the greedy landowners who, by going over to sheep-farming, were driving unemployed workers into poverty and crime.

Today the connection between religion and politics, for instance, would be questioned. In 1983 Conor Cruise O'Brien the Irish diplomat, wrote in the *Observer*:

> I think religion is best kept out of politics. The separation of Church and State represents an advance in civilisation. Places that have a great deal of religion in their politics, like Ireland and Iran, do not seem much better for it.

Of course religion can embitter politics, but whether the preacher can ignore manifest injustice, dishonesty and crude materialism in politics is another matter. When politicians begin to grumble about the Church interfering, it usually means the Church is right!

What applies to politics applies also to science and economics. A Christian biologist who happened to disapprove of abortion and tampered with the results of his research in order to prove his point would be a dishonest scientist and a bad Christian. A Christian economist who rigged his figures in order to make the needs of the Third World even more horrifying than they really are, would be open to the same criticism. None the less, Christian leaders cannot ignore increasingly arrogant practices in the field of genetics. Nor can they be silent where powerful corporations condemn the vulnerable to desperate poverty or even disease by their practices. Injustice and exploitation are as much an affront to the Christian conscience as they were to Amos.

Amos can be a chilling companion in our spiritual quest, but his righteous indignation has its place alongside our compassion. And it is always good to be reminded that the forgiveness of God is costly and not to be taken for granted. Our deeds have consequences for others, and for the Christian those deeds – much the same as those condemned by Amos – once erected a cross for the Son of God. Only through the suffering of God in Christ is there freedom for us.

Questions
1. Have you ever failed to be truthful with family or friends because you feared to hurt them?

2. Think of ways in which the criticisms made by Amos in chapter 5 apply to our world today.

3. Do you agree that politics and religion should always be separate?

4. Some geneticists today contemplate changing the genetic structure of human beings in order to eliminate vicious or immoral tendencies. Is this justified?

5. Is it a legitimate criticism of Amos to say that his prophecy lacks hope and love?

6. Discuss the view that city and town life are more morally unhealthy than simpler and less sophisticated living would be.

7. Why is it that quite decent people can be unjust or allow injustice to be done in their name?

8. Look carefully at the phrase 'Deeds have consequences.' Do you agree?

Chapter 3

Isaiah and the Holiness of God

The prophet did not recoil from his vision with shuddering awe, as if he had become aware of that which was unintelligible and 'wholly other' ... On the contrary, his response was personal and moral; he confessed his sin and offered his life in the Lord's service.

E. W. Heaton, *The Old Testament Prophets*

God is not a projection into infinity of the nicest person we have ever met. He comes to meet us out of the beyond as the Holy Other. As one of the saints said, 'He emerges from dazzling darkness.' When we talk about God we are talking about an unfathomable mystery.

Colin Morris, *Starting from Scratch*

Passage for study: Isaiah 6

The holiness of God

We have already seen that the note of fear played a central part in Hebrew religion, as indeed it does in all early religion. Unsophisticated societies are loth to come into too close contact with gods. They are thought to be dangerous beings. Twice in the life of Jacob the patriarch was alarmed by the evidence of the divine presence, and on the second occasion he marvelled that he had met God face to face and was still alive to tell the tale (Genesis 28:10 and 32:30). In Exodus 19 God actually warned Moses to keep his people away from the sacred mountain. These are only two of numerous incidents in the Old Testament.

This power of which they were so apprehensive is part of what they discerned as the holiness of God. And it is still part of the human experience. The word 'holiness', however, has widened its meaning.

If you were asked what the word 'holy' meant to you, a vision of a church with its centuries of worship and prayer might spring to your mind. Or the special atmosphere of a Communion service, or a special kind of goodness which humbles you might seem more appropriate. All these responses point in the right direction. They are looking at a quality which belongs to God and which makes him qualitatively different from ourselves.

The word 'holy' literally means 'separate' or 'set aside' and, therefore, what is set aside for God is described as holy. A minister or a building may be holy for that reason. But that would also assume that God's holiness, his distinctive goodness, was to be found in the life of the minister or the church.

Isaiah and his vision

Isaiah was a native of Judah and his career stretched from 735 BC until well into the next century. He must have heard of the destruction of the Northern Kingdom and was in Jerusalem when it was besieged by the Assyrians. Happily for him he was not alive when his beloved city was destroyed by Babylon.

He was the only prophet who influenced kings. He guided King Hezekiah very effectively because the latter did try to cleanse Judah of idolatry and evil practices like child sacrifice.

The dating of the vision is important. Uzziah had been a great king but unhappily power and popularity went to his head. He wanted to have the power of the priests as well as his own – much like Henry VIII who succeeded in making himself head of the Church in England. Uzziah burned incense in the Temple – a task reserved for the priests. He was immediately stricken with leprosy and died soon afterwards.

You may well think the punishment was a bit 'over the top'. You would not expect a British Prime Minister to be so severely punished for trying to take over the duties of the Archbishop of Canterbury. But pride in the face of God was very serious in the eyes of the ancient world and it merited dire punishment.

When Isaiah remembers the day of his vision he remembers with sadness the great king who had died that year. Isaiah had probably been in a mood of great sorrow at the downfall of one who may well have been his youthful hero. One commentator has likened Isaiah's mood to that of men and women present at the funeral of Abraham Lincoln or, much later, at the funeral of Martin Luther King. Hope seems to have been destroyed for them as for Isaiah.

The vision itself almost defeats Isaiah's powers of description, despite its vividness. The objects in the vision were all there in the Temple. There was a bronze image of a serpent traditionally ascribed to Moses, an altar of incense and tongs. Moreover the purification of vessels in worship by touching them with live coals was not unknown. These elements are in Isaiah's vision. However, it is the deeper significance of the vision which is most important. It tells us something about the meaning of holiness as it touches human feelings, enlightens the mind and challenges the conscience.

Holiness and feeling

The description which Isaiah gives of his feelings is one of trembling awe. The whole building seems to shake and his consciousness is displaced. E. W. Heaton seems to dispute this in the quotation at the head of this study. That there was a deeply moral response is not to be doubted, but that need not exclude the kind of religious experience which is one of the trembling wonder and awe.

You may feel that if this is holiness, you have never experienced it in your worship. For instance, you would not describe your church at 11am next Sunday as Gerrard Tersteegen describes it in a hymn translated by John Wesley (*H&P* 531). Wesley's original version reads:

> Lo, God is here, let us adore!
> And own how dreadful is this place,
> Let all within us feel his power,
> And silent bow before his face.

We do not generally want to think of God in this way, but rather as a close friend. The image of Jesus and of the Father he revealed to the people is more central to our worship. The version of the hymn in *Hymns & Psalms* has toned down the word 'dreadful' to 'awe-inspiring', perhaps because of this reaction.

Yet the element of awe and wonder is justified, and when Colin Morris speaks of God emerging from 'dazzling darkness' he is rightly emphasising an element in religious experience which is important. Perhaps that is what is meant by Tersteegen when he completes his verse:

> Who know his power, his grace who prove,
> Serve him with awe, with reverence love.

The love we owe God must be combined with the reverence that derives from awe and wonder. The German scholar Rudolf Otto called this feeling 'numinous' and he regarded it as basic to all religion.

It is one of the primary human responses. It is possible to be so moved by great music that our consciousness of our surroundings is dislocated. Majestic scenery can have both a forbidding aspect and offer us overwhelming beauty. I well remember my father standing in tears in the Pass of Glencoe, quite oblivious of other people. I have met young parents who confess to an experience of almost unbearable wonder and awe when they gazed at their first baby. Perhaps these are all ways in which God's holiness touches us.

I also believe that places where men and women have worshipped God over long periods of years have a capacity to disturb. My wife finds Winchester Cathedral deeply disturbing and we both remember vividly one moonlit night when we drove through the village of Avebury, which is set in a stone circle. We both began to tremble and we stopped outside the village to recover. That ancient site clearly had deep religious associations even if they were not Christian.

You may be able to remember moments when a verse from the Bible gripped you as never before, or a prayer or a hymn, quite familiar to you, suddenly enveloped you so that you would have staked your life on its truth. Just very occasionally you may have felt a joyous communion with God as if you were alone with him, even in a packed church. These can be moments when holiness really grasps us.

You may think it does not often happen. Colin Morris has suggested that this may be part of the mercy of God – because an overwhelming presence 'paralyses action'. I think I know what he means. As a 20-year old student I was taking a service at Woodstock. Two minutes before my sermon I noticed an elderly minister in the back corner of the church and realised with a shock that it was an ex-President of the Wesleyan Methodist Conference. He was very kind, but he was all too obviously *there*, and I was green, as green could be! God spares us that kind of paralysis.

But sometimes we miss the experience because our worship is too self-centred. We sing an unfamiliar tune, or attend an unfamiliar form of service. The sermon displeases us. All our spikes come out and we become grumbling worshippers. Do we miss those moments of holiness because we expect too much of our fellows and too little of God?

Holiness and thinking
Isaiah's vision contains the anthem which we call the Sanctus and it speaks of the whole earth being filled with God's glory. There is here a realisation that God's glory, his 'worth' is beyond our human understanding, that we never can fully grasp what God is in himself. It is a mystery. The medieval mystic Richard Rolle expresses it thus:

> There is nothing so sweet as loving Christ, and because this is so let us not inquire too closely into matters we earthlings cannot possibly understand. In the Father's house there will be clearer light if we bring our whole heart to the loving of God.

The vision of holiness calls for intellectual humility. We have to acknowledge the mystery that is at the heart of the universe. That does not place an embargo on the kind of knowledge which our God-given minds may discover; it simply restrains us from claiming that our knowledge is infallible, with all the disastrous consequences that our intellectual arrogance can have when it handles modern technology.

That same humility must also apply to religion. Paul Tillich has pointed out how easily we slip into the habit of thinking that we possess God. We think our beliefs give us complete knowledge of God, that our Bible tells us everything about him. We think that our particular denomination has the monopoly of truth. We close our minds to God just as easily as we close our minds to the truth which others possess.

Holiness and the conscience

It is, of course, the conscience of Isaiah which is most powerfully affected by his vision. He feels unworthy, quite unable to live in the presence of God. He feels his own sinfulness and that of his people. It is a marvellous transformation of sheer wonder into a moral experience.

It is the wholeness of God which is in such vivid contrast to his own sinful and divided self. Perhaps we can understand it if we think of those moments when our vision of Christ has had the same effect as it did upon the people of the gospels – the bullying Zaccheus, the proud Nathanael, the sceptic Thomas. Sometimes it seems like a peace at the heart of things which is in vivid contrast with the conflict around us and in our own hearts. Sometimes it is a love which seems the opposite of our own self-centredness – even when we are trying hard to be unselfish. Sometimes we feel that Christ is totally to be trusted whereas we cannot easily trust ourselves.

But, as with Isaiah, there is always hope. The moment of healing is never far away from our discernment of God's wholeness if in humility we are open to him. For that is the great paradox of faith, that God shows his holiness, his wholeness most of all by his mercy, by that healing which shares his wholeness with us, and which sends us out in his service.

A postscript
I conclude with some words of Simone Weil, the French mystic, speaking of God's holiness:

> We cannot take one step towards him. We cannot walk vertically. We can only turn our eyes towards him. We do not have to search for him. We only have to change the direction in which we are looking. It is for him to search for us. We must be happy in the knowledge that he is infinitely beyond our reach. Thus we can be certain that the evil in us in no way sullies the divine purity and perfection.

In other words, whatever horrors we perpetrate, however far we fall away from Christian living, God's holy love is like an impregnable fortress. He can never be undermined or defeated.

Isaiah would have understood those words of Simone Weil. He encouraged his people to trust an invincible, holy God and when he called on his people to repent, it was in the name of the holy God who had reached out and healed him.

Questions
1. Whilst we are right to create a friendly atmosphere in our churches, do we lose something important in the process?

2. 'One effect of being surrounded by so many technological wonders is that we tend to lose our capacity for wonder.' Is this true and if so does it have an adverse effect upon our religious life?

3. J. B. Phillips wrote a book entitled *Your God is Too Small*. Have we made God too small?

4. What special qualities in Jesus seem to justify the word 'holy' as applied to him? Are they in any way different from the quality of Isaiah's vision?

5. Do you think that it is possible for a place – a church, a home, or even an open-air setting – to become 'holy' through long years of prayer and the practice of Christian love?

6. If a member of your group is familiar with the work of T. S. Eliot, let them introduce a little of the poem 'Little Gidding' which dwells on the holiness of places sanctified by Christian love.

7. Share any experience, or find a hymn, poem or prose passage which has helped you to understand the meaning of holiness.

Chapter 4

Micah – The Prophet of True Worship

> To worship well is to live well. [A person's] whole being, physical, mental and spiritual, is required to co-operate in this redemptive task.
>
> Evelyn Underhill, *Worship*

Passages for study: The central passage is Micah 6:6-8 and chapters 2, 4:3f, 5:2f and 6:9-11 will be noted.

About Micah
Like Amos he was a poor countryman, though not from the wilderness but from a rich and fertile countryside. He was probably a young man when Isaiah of Jerusalem was an aged prophet. So he knew what had happened to the Northern Kingdom.

He is not just an echo of Amos. Although he too can thunder judgements against his people and is just as angry about social injustice, Micah has something more to say which is nearer to the message of Hosea. He dwells on the nature of worship and the roots of moral behaviour.

Worship and life
His basic question is stated in 6:6

> With what shall I come before the Lord and bow myself before God on high?

As we shall see, he combines duty to God with moral obedience. But that does not mean that worship is downgraded. Worship and life belong together as the words of Evelyn Underhill above suggest.

For Micah moral behaviour is essential if we are to approach God rightly. But that does not mean that morality can be divorced from that religious obligation. Many anthropologists today propose a secular origin for morality. Their explanation is that, since human beings co-operated for defence, for hunting and for the rearing and protection of their young, they began to develop a simple morality in order to keep the peace in their small communities.

Early peoples, however, were very conscious of living in a world that was not their own. They were dependent on an environment that could leave them without rain, could destroy their crops or herds, and could visit them with disease and calamity. They felt presences behind the world – gods whose favour they tried to secure by rites and sacrifices. And their morality, too, had often a basic religious sanction. They believed they owed an obedience of a kind to their gods who looked after the welfare of their clans and tribes.

Although Micah's message marks a sharp advance on that early form of religion, he is not dispensing with religion. What he is saying is that sin cannot be blotted out by sacrifices (6:7). To approach God in worship we must bring moral obedience as the principal quality he requires. Moreover Micah is very emphatic that poor religious teaching and leadership can undermine the life of a nation (3:5).

It is important, however, not to confuse Micah's assertion with a very modern view that the word 'Christian' is a synonym for decency, neighbourliness and respectable behaviour. God is in the centre of Micah's universe and neither community nor individual rights can displace him. That alone is a challenge to the modern view.

The demand for justice

The first claim that Micah makes is that men should 'do justly'. Justice is God's order of things and we can only participate in that order – his kingdom – by doing justly.

Like Amos he gives vivid examples of what injustice entails. For instance:

> Alas for those who devise wickedness and evil deeds on their beds! When the morning dawns, they perform it, because it is in their power. They covet fields, and seize them; houses, and take them away; they oppress householder and house, people and their inheritance.

This passage (2:1-2) paints a lurid picture of lawlessness on the part of the rich and powerful.

The same impression is gained from 2:8f where daylight robbery and the eviction of women and children from their homes is described. He accuses his people of hating good and loving evil (3:2). Then in 6:10f, like Hosea, he accuses the merchants of cheating by using measures that are false and of living by being 'economical with the truth'.

So angry is Micah at the injustice he sees in Judah that his condemnation seems to embrace the whole nation, and gives the impression that the people are totally depraved and devoid of any concern for justice.

Most Christians today would demur. Although it is often masked by selfishness there is in human beings an instinctive desire for fairness and justice which expresses itself very early in life. Schoolchildren will accept rebuke and punishment if they believe that it is fair. In fact they sometimes appear to prefer fairness to kindness. Kindness seems more difficult to regulate and less disinterested and impartial than fairness.

Adults might express the idea differently but they believe justice should have priority, even though what they may think of as just could be very defective and even unjust.

That very instinct, however, is in conflict with faith at times. Paul Tillich has called attention to what he calls the Riddle of Inequality. 'Why,' he says, 'is one person born to desperate poverty and another to affluence, and why is the power to gain more out of his human life given to one being more than to another?'

That would apply not just to possessions, but to physical disabilities, limited intelligence, and the disadvantages of a poor home.

It is not a complete answer to that dilemma, but it is perhaps true that the instinct for justice of which we have just spoken, however weakly it seems to function, is God's way of seeking, through us, to right the inequalities and injustices which nature itself and the structure of human life create. This is the way he has chosen and we are answerable for our response. That is Micah's message.

If we try to apply it to ourselves, clearly we must not be afraid to challenge injustice and to support those who strive to remedy what is manifestly unjust. But also we must take care that we do not use our own gifts and powers to manipulate or degrade others – whether they be workmates, neighbours, or members of our own family. We might be shocked if we saw how often we are unjust to our husband or wife, let alone when we make snap judgements about the motives and behaviour of people we do not really know. And we can be unjust by our silence, when, for instance, we fail to protest about some racist sentiment expressed by a friend or colleague just because we do not want to offend them.

To do justly means having a self-restraint born of faith and the grace of God.

The demand for compassion

The Hebrew word here translated mercy means rather more than a simple willingness to forgive. It carries the additional meaning of compassion.

Compassion is, with justice, the essential basis of human relationships, because where compassion is lacking trust will be destroyed. In 7:5-6 Micah declares that one of the worst features of life in Judah is broken relationships:

> Put no trust in a friend, have no confidence in a loved one; guard the doors of your mouth from her who lies in your embrace; for the son treats the father with contempt, the daughter rides up against her mother, the daughter-in-law against her mother-in-law; your enemies are members of your own household.

By contrast, in 4:6-7, Micah depicts God as showing compassion:

> In that day, says the Lord, I will assemble the lame and gather those who have been driven away, and those whom I have afflicted. The lame I will make the remnant, and those who were cast off, a strong nation.

Here is the pattern for compassion.

Compassion is also one way in which God, through us, relieves life's inequalities and injustices. It is more easily stifled than the instinct for fairness and sometimes seems to wither away, but it is surprising how it can suddenly emerge in a very hardened individual. We need to understand its implications.

It is not always easy to exercise compassion because people in quite grievous need sometimes put up a barrier of perverse pride, believing that this is self-respect. But we must try.

Nor is pity enough. Compassion means 'suffering with' and that is difficult to achieve. Blaise Pascal has pointed up the contrast:

> Pity for the unfortunate does not run contrary to desire. On the contrary we are very glad to show such evidence of friendship and win a reputation for sympathy without giving anything in return.

How different is compassion. I remember hearing of a distinguished Sri Lankan minister and scholar who won the trust of a mentally handicapped girl, and by telling her Bible stories with exquisite simplicity and loving patience, helped her to feel the reality of God's love for her. This is the meaning of compassion.

Micah, however, says we are to 'love mercy'. It is possible to be kind for all sorts of reasons. We may want the good opinion of others. We may be simply respecting the feelings of friends and family. Or we may have inherited a set of decent attitudes. But when passions are aroused, or our security or family interests seem threatened, then only a genuine love of goodness, of compassion and mercy can be proof against passion or fear.

A sad illustration makes the point. A very generous supporter of Oxfam and Christian Aid came to grief when the prospect of having coloured families in her immediate neighbourhood turned her into a fulminating and angry protestor. To be compassionate was not enough. It needed a love of compassion. And that is a gift of God.

The demand for humility

Humility is not markedly a virtue in the Old Testament as it is in the New Testament. It is found more frequently in the Psalms than anywhere else (see for instance Psalm 9:12, 10:12, 34:2, 69:32).

Humility is not easy to define. It is not a spurious modesty which leads us to be self-deprecating in the hope that God or one of our fellows will praise us. Nor is it a helpless clinging to God, expecting him to make our decisions for us and to cope with our trifling problems.

Perhaps one way of defining humility is as that quality which distinguishes people who do not take themselves too seriously. God wants us to take our obligations seriously, but not ourselves. We should be able to laugh at our own foibles without feeling secretly hurt. We should not be worrying whether we are deemed to be important. We should be able to rejoice in the joy of others without envy breaking in. We should be glad to see God's justice and compassion touching the world about us. And best of all feel that the love of God for us is sufficient for us.

What an idea! How out of reach it seems! Yet I have met people just like that and have been greatly enriched by the experience.

The prophets and the future

The four prophets we have just surveyed had a profound influence on Judaism. In our next chapter we shall see how they influenced the Law. Together with the book of Deuteronomy they laid the foundation of the prophetic tradition which still influenced the teaching of the synagogues and the beliefs of the Pharisees in the time of Jesus. Their criticisms of the priestly rites and Temple customs were often referred to by thoughtful rabbis. And, of course, they were the foundation of our Lord's own moral teaching.

Questions

1. Micah appears to insist that morality is the first requirement of worship. Does this fit your own idea? What else might be required?

2. Which do you consider to be the most important for society and for the individual Christian: justice or mercy?

3. A friend of mine once said, 'If God expects us to be just, should he not have arranged that there are fewer inequalities to start with?' What do you think?

4. What do you consider to be the most shameful injustice of our time? How far can it be connected with a failure of religious faith?

5. How important is it to love goodness for its own sake? Talk over some ways in which ordinary decency is liable to break down under pressure.

6. Is humility a desirable virtue in the world as it is? List some practical ways in which it is important.

7. How far does contemporary morality still derive from Christian sources? If there has been a perceptible decline in Christian influence, in what particular areas is it most obvious?

Chapter 5

The Hebrews
A People of the Law

I have gone the whole round of creation; I saw and I
spoke I, a work of God's hand for that purpose,
received in my brain. And pronounced on the rest of
his handiwork – returned him again His creation's
approval or censure; I spoke as I saw I report as a man
may of God's work – all's love, yet all's law.

Robert Browning, The Ring and The Book

Passages for study: This study is based principally on
excerpts from Deuteronomy together with Psalm 19:7f.
The references will be given in the text.

Deuteronomy and the eighth-century prophets
There is no better way of assessing the ultimate influence
of Amos, Hosea, Isaiah of Jerusalem and Micah than by
perusing the pages of Deuteronomy. The Jews were a
people of the Law and it was in a way the 'badge' of the
nation. In Deuteronomy we discover moral precepts more
sensitive than any other laws of that age.

The writer of 2 Kings (22:8f) tells a story of how, at the
beginning of the reign of Josiah, the young king gave
orders for the repair of the Temple. During the work, a
priest named Hilkiah found a scroll on which were written
laws which had been long since forgotten or ignored.
Josiah immediately inaugurated a reformation on the basis
of those Laws.

Scholars assume that this was Deuteronomy, or part of it.
Parts of the present book may well have been in that scroll.
But it is also likely that sections of the book were added,

either in Josiah's reign or later, incorporating precepts and laws which reflect the teaching of the eighth-century prophets. We shall try to show just how much the Law owes to our four messengers.

Law then and now
The Anglo-Saxon nations are quite justly proud of their legal systems but the underlying principles are very different from those of the ancient Hebrews. The greater part of our common law has grown up over many centuries simply by trial and error in the courts, but the last three centuries have added a mass of legislation enacted by Parliaments or Congress. So most law is the will of the nation expressed through its elected representatives. Laws have been enacted to ensure the security and order of national life, to protect the rights of various groups of citizens, to promote the economic well-being of the community and to educate its children. If Parliament is ready to enact a law and public opinion will accept it, there is no authority which can veto that law.

By contrast the Hebrews believed that law was the will of God. A brief glance at the Decalogue or Ten Commandments reveals the great difference between then and now.

The prohibition of murder, theft and perjury are common to any civilised legal system and a breach of them is a criminal offence. In the Decalogue they also offend God.

Adultery is still a criminal offence is some cultures but, although it is frowned upon by some sections of Western society, it is a moral rather than a legal matter. For the modern Muslim, as for the ancient Hebrew, it is a crime.

Even more distant from modern legal enactment is the injunction to honour parents. Whilst considered desirable, it is a matter of moral principle. In Deuteronomy disobedience to a father is punishable by death.

The prohibition of coveting or envy could not be enforced by external law.

Finally the first four commandments are entirely within the realm of religion and no laws exist in most Western countries which even attempt to regulate what is regarded as the individual's private concern.

In Deuteronomy you will find mingled together criminal laws, remedies for disagreement between individuals, demands for social co-operation as well as moral prohibitions and regulations for religious rites and duties. The Jews did not differentiate between criminal, civil, moral and religious law. It was all the will of God.

Indeed, Oesterley and Robinson have said that for the Jews God was Law. God himself lived according to law:

> They might have described Yahweh as omnipotent, but they would have said that omnipotence was limited by self-consistency. It was possible to know what Yahweh would do, for he could not be false to himself. His will might be absolute but it was reliable; he did not change, and what was good in his sight today would not appear evil tomorrow.

The same consistency was to be found in the Law and could be demanded of God's people. That was the prophetic message and it is enshrined in Deuteronomy.

Deuteronomy and the prophets

The laws are centred in a narrative about Moses and his injunctions to the people of Israel. It is likely that the Decalogue in chapter 5 and the instructions concerning respect for the Law in chapter 6 were traditions older than the present book. So were the regulations concerning the Passover and other feasts in chapter 16.

We begin to see the prophetic influence strongly in chapter 13 where in verses 1-5 there is the threat of capital punishment for false prophets. Compare this with Hosea 4:4f and Micah 3:5. In this connection idolatry is also prohibited and in 13:6-7 the enticement to idolatry by family or friends, which the prophets must often have noticed, is roundly condemned.

It is in the moral sphere, however, that the relationship between the prophets and Deuteronomy is most clearly seen.

Thus the robbery and seizure of other people's property condemned by both Amos and Micah is prohibited in 19:14.

Perjury and false witness noted by Amos in 5:10 is condemned in 19:15-18.

Pledges given by borrowers as security for a loan were often misused by the lenders and this is condemned by Amos in 2:8 and prohibited in Deuteronomy 24:6-13. It is particularly forbidden to take as a pledge anything like a millstone which would deprive a man of his living.

Selling people into slavery is a common complaint of Amos and this is prohibited in 24:14f.

Cheating, which is mentioned in Hosea 12:7f and Micah 6:10 and 7:1-4 is prohibited in Deuteronomy 25:13-16.

On the positive side there are laws which seek to encourage compassion. For instance chapter 15 prescribes a year of release when debts shall be cancelled and slaves freed.

In chapter 19 'cities of refuge' are set up, very like the medieval sanctuaries, to which people who accidentally killed another person could flee to find protection from angry relatives.

The regulations for military service are also very humane (20:5-8). Those who have built new houses, or planted new vineyards, or are newly married or are fearful are to be allowed to go home! Although this is not mentioned anywhere in the prophets, it echoes the demand for compassion which the prophets make.

There are also laws providing for the poor which insist that farmers should leave part of their crops of cereals and grapes for gleaning (24:19-22). Foreigners are also protected (24:17-18) and there is even protection for young animals and their mothers (22:6-7). Once more these are in the spirit of the four prophets.

In total the moral and social laws of Deuteronomy display a concern for justice and for compassion which helped to prepare the Jewish people for their destiny as the nation to whom God would send his Son with a gospel of divine love and compassion.

A serious problem

Deuteronomy, however, raises a problem which was to be the single most serious question posed in the Old Testament and which remains for many people today an insoluble enigma. It is the problem of why the good and righteous suffer.

Deuteronomy takes it for granted that prosperity and well-being are the just reward of the righteous, and suffering the just reward for the wicked. This is repeated a number of times, notably in chapters 8 and 11 and again at the end of the book in chapters 27-29. Those who keep the Law are to be blessed. Those who disobey will be cursed. This is encapsulated in 11:26-28:

> See, I am setting before you today a blessing and a curse: the blessing, if you obey the commandments of the Lord your God that I am commanding you today; and the course, if you do not obey the commandments of the Lord your God, but turn from the way that I am commanding you today, to follow other gods that you have not known.

It is not difficult to see the influence of the prophets here, particularly Amos and Micah. It is implied in Amos 3:6 where we read:

> Does disaster befall a city, unless the Lord has done it?

Again and again the disasters of the past are ascribed to the judgement of God on Israel's disobedience (Amos 4:6-12).

This does not seem to have been a problem as long as it was national prosperity and calamity which were regarded as the blessing and judgement of God. As H. H. Rowley puts it:

> The thought of Deuteronomy was primarily of the nation, for it was never the teaching of any part of the Bible that individual fortune and merit were rigidly bound together and perfectly matched.

But when the individual began to look at his personal prosperity and good fortune as the blessing of God and personal calamities as divine judgements, then the way was open for protest and questioning, for exploration of the fact and experience of suffering by prophets and other writers like the writer of the book of Job. In that sense the years immediately before the fall of Jerusalem and those of the Exile and its aftermath were some of the most spiritually troubled and spiritually creative in the history of humankind.

The quality of the Law

Psalm 19 is a hymn of praise to God the Creator and to God the giver of the Law. Although it is ascribed to David, the wonder of Creation and the deeply spiritual understanding of the Law would seem to place it much later – certainly later than Deuteronomy. Moffatt's translation is particularly helpful here.

The Authorised Version of the Bible speaks of the Law as 'perfect, converting the soul'. Moffatt speaks of it as a sound law with the power to revive the life of the spirit (v7). The implication is that when men and women begin to drift morally through loss of self-control, perverse decisions and lack of moral stamina, the discipline of the sound Law can restore a firmness and purpose to their lives. Christians would place more stress on the grace of

God, but there can be little doubt that the discipline of sound moral values is also imperative.

The Law also 'makes wise the simple'. Moffatt speaks of instructing the open minded (v7). Here the educational importance of the Law, which was the basis of the training of children in the synagogue is emphasised. Notice, however, the necessity of an open mind, a readiness to learn and to put effort into the learning which is as vital now as ever, for adults as well as children.

In the Authorised Version the Law is said to 'rejoice the heart'. Moffatt simply says it is a joy to the heart (v8). Here the value of the Law is stressed. The Jews do not simply obey the Law, they cherish it. They find joy in their obedience. How far is that true for Christians today? Are we sometimes ready enough to accept the claims of discipleship on our conscience and to obey, but find that it is a joyless exercise, a burden to be faithfully borne, but scarcely a joy?

Then we read that the Law, and the obedience men and women owe to it, is clean, enlightening the eyes or, as Moffatt puts it, it is clear, easily understood and so is a light to the mind (v8). There can be no excuse for injustice on the part of God's children because in the Law they have a firm guide to fairness and justice. How Micah would have rejoiced in that verse of the psalm!

Finally in v12-14 we find that the Law is seen not just as a firm discipline for outward actions but as a challenge to the conscience. This is a deeply spiritual interpretation of the Law. The Authorised Version speaks of 'secret faults'. Moffatt speaks of 'faults unknown'. This could mean faults which are not only secret from the world, but of which we are ourselves unaware. They may be unintentional but are the result of ignorance, foolishness or carelessness. This is confirmed by v13 which speaks of wilful sins, disobedience with eyes wide open to the consequences. The concluding prayer, so well known to Christians, is an apt response of the Jew to the Law he cherished.

Two brief reflections
Today religious faith and values do not influence law making as they once did – and indeed still do in some Catholic and all Muslim countries. It is, however, difficult to see how law can be used to enforce private morality without tragic consequences. An atmosphere of fear can so easily arise and grave injustices occur because the law is interpreted in an inhumane fashion. One has only to remember the pregnant girls who were left homeless by strict parents and the women who were ostracised and broken because of a moral lapse which had ended their marriage, to wonder whether the kind of cast iron and rigid framework which, for instance, reigns in very orthodox Muslim lands can be an expression of Christian morality.

On the other hand a society which has no respect for the law is hardly a civilised one. It may be that our rightful recognition that there can be legitimate differences of judgement on moral issues, and even on the justice of some laws, has undermined our readiness to accept that our obligations are as important as our rights. The Jews as people of the Law did not make that mistake – and it was to them that Christ came.

Questions
1. Deuteronomic Law seeks to enforce morality as well as civil obedience. Is this desirable in any society or are we right to treat crime differently from immorality?

2. 'The only way to educate children in acceptable moral and social behaviour is through the practice of living in a community which affords them adequate respect.' Do you agree?

3. Read Deuteronomy 21:18-21 and 24:5-7 and 10-22. How far can the laws be said to be humane? Has the Christian community made any advance on this?

4. How far is your conscience guided
   a) by the law of our country
   b) by the values of our particular time
   c) by laws you have derived from the Bible
   d) by inner communion with Christ?

5. I have referred above to times when Christian discipleship is a joyless exercise. Why do you think this happens?

6. In the Sermon on the Mount (Matt. 5:19-20) Jesus appears to cherish the Jewish Law as a great ideal, but in Mark 2 and 3 he appears to defy it. What can we learn from his attitude to the Sabbath Law which is applicable to all law?

7. Psalm 19 appears to make a distinction between unintentional and deliberate sin. Is this legitimate?

Chapter 6

Jeremiah (1)
The Origins of Personal Religion

My soul was exceeding sorrowful at the love
feast to find so little love and so much dispute.
I spoke as healingly as I could, declared what
God had done for the colliers, put them in
remembrance of his work begun in them by our
ministry . . . concluded with expostulation, how
injuriously our brethren had dealt with us, by
dissuading all from hearing us, and hindering
as much as in them lay, the farther course of our
ministry.

Charles Wesley, *Journal,* 13th April 1740

Passages for study: Jeremiah is a long and in places
repetitive prophecy. The principal passages referred to
below are chapters 1 and 2:1-13, 17:9-18, 18, 19, 20:1-2 and
7-13, 22:13-17, 23:1-2 and 9-14, 26:1-11.

About Jeremiah
The very name Jeremiah is associated with pessimism. Yet
that is only one part of the prophet's message. During the
years just before 586 BC when Jerusalem was destroyed by
the Chaldeans, Jeremiah was justifiably pessimistic. But,
as we shall see in the next study, there is also hopefulness,
though it must have been difficult to sustain.

Jeremiah is a reluctant prophet. In 1:1-5 we are told that
he is the son of Hilkiah, probably the priest who found the
scroll in the Temple. He is completely shattered by his call
to be a prophet and protests that he is but a child. Whether
this means that he is only a youth or simply inexperienced

is not certain. However, when like Isaiah, his lips have been touched by God he accepts his destiny (1:9).

Jeremiah had much in common with Hosea. They both made sacrifices – Hosea accepted domestic bitterness, Jeremiah remained unmarried, although he would have loved to have had children. Both of them hated to seem unpatriotic. Both hated to predict the destruction of their beloved city. In 1:13-16 a picture is drawn of the threat from the north i.e. from the Chaldeans, and it is not difficult to see why, like Hosea, he would find such a message constantly repeated very unpalatable.

The end of chapter 1 suggests that Jeremiah placed his trust in God. He was promised that he would be defended 'like a fortified city' against the kings of Judah and the leading nobility and priests. And, despite moments when he seemed to be in danger of losing his life, he did survive. He was left in Jerusalem after its fall and then taken by refugees to Egypt where eventually he died.

Jeremiah's message
The prophecy is one of mingled pleas and warnings.

Chapter 2:1-13 is an example of Jeremiah's pleading which could be compared with the winsome plea of Hosea.

The people are bidden to remember the distant days when God led them through the wilderness from Egypt. They had been protected from evil (2:2-4).

God, through the prophet, then asks why the people have deserted him. What evil have they found in him that they should have turned to idolatry? (2:5-8). They have abandoned Yahweh, who is their glory, for worthless idols (v11). Then in v13 this desertion is compared to someone turning their back on a spring of fresh water and trying to live on water kept in leaking cisterns.

The plea is repeated in the following chapter, especially in 3:12-14, and subsequently nearly a dozen times in the prophecy.

The prophecy contains judgements against all the surrounding nations, but it is Israel's treachery which seems so grievous to both the prophet and his God. In addition to idolatry, which is the main complaint of Jeremiah, two charges are made which are reminiscent of the eighth century prophets.

For instance in 22:13f a warning is given to those who build houses, the cost of which had been defrayed by dishonesty and oppression, probably by forcing a poorer neighbour to work without payment. In v17 covetousness, murder, oppression and violence are listed as the sins of the people.

Chapter 23 contains severe warnings against the pastors and prophets. The pastors by their leadership have led the people astray. They will be replaced (23:1-4). Then the prophets are accused of lying, of strengthening the hands of evil-doers and proclaiming their own opinions rather than God's word (23:14-16). They may be confident that they are immune to trouble but they will be punished (23:19-21).

There are a number of acted parables in the prophecy, in which Jeremiah, by dramatic actions, reinforces his message in a way which will capture the attention of the people. In two of them Jeremiah issues a terrible warning.

In chapter 18 Jeremiah has a vision at a potter's house where he sees the potter scrap an unsatisfactory pot and then reshape it. In v6 he hears the voice of God likening himself to the potter:

> Can I not do with you, O house of Israel, just as this potter has done? says the Lord. Just like the clay in the potter's hand, so are you in my hand.

Jeremiah is ordered to take this warning to the people (18:11). They have already been warned again and again, but have not heeded and have instead followed their own evil inclinations (v12). Once more it is idolatry which is denounced as the great evil (v15). They will be punished by being scattered because God will turn his back on them in the day of calamity, when they are attacked by the Chaldeans and their allies (v17).

The people's response is simply to plot against the prophet. Jeremiah is angry because he has been so cruelly treated and in a prayer he begs that God will punish them with famine, military defeat and massacre (v19-22). The tone of this passage, and especially the unforgiving spirit of v23, compares very adversely with that of the crucified Christ, and indeed with that of some modern Christians who have undergone torture and cruelty in prison and concentration camps.

The next chapter contains the second acted parable. Here Jeremiah goes to the valley of Hinnom, a place where the people have made human sacrifices. There he proclaims the destruction of Jerusalem and as a sign he breaks an earthenware pot, telling them that the calamity of Jerusalem will be the result of their wickedness. (In fact Jeremiah's action was never forgotten and when Jerusalem was rebuilt the valley of Hinnom became a vast incinerator for the rubbish of the city. It was called Gehenna – a word which became a synonym for hell.)

To an ancient people, especially one given to idolatry, the breaking of the pot seems like witchcraft. They think that Jeremiah is himself putting a curse on the city which will inevitably come true. Instead of recognising a warning from God for what it is, they are simply incensed against the prophet. From that time onwards the king and leaders regarded Jeremiah as a traitor in the pay of the Chaldeans. Such is their blindness.

The suffering of the prophet and its consequences

Jeremiah suffers outwardly from the hostility of the authorities and the people. He is placed in the stocks (20:1), thrown into prison (chapter 26) and lowered into a miry pit where he would have died of starvation but for the intervention of a court servant named Ebed Melech who persuades the king to rescue him. In a moving story (38:7-13), the rescue is accomplished with wonderful compassion for Jeremiah in his weakened state, the servant using old cloths to prevent the ropes from cutting into the prophet's armpits.

Jeremiah is often angry with his people as we saw above. But he is also very rebellious against God from time to time. One of the most tortured passages in the Bible – outside the Book of Job – occurs in chapter 20:7-8. The delay in the fulfilment of Jeremiah's prophecy causes him to charge God with deviousness:

O Lord, you have enticed me, and I was enticed; you have overpowered me, and you have prevailed. I have become a laughing stock all day long; everyone mocks me. For whenever I speak, I must cry out, I must shout, 'Violence and destruction!' For the word of the Lord has become for me a reproach and derision all day long.

Momentarily he resolves to make no more prophecies for God but then:

> If I say, 'I will not mention him, or speak any more in his name,' then within me there is something like a burning fire shut up in my bones; I am weary with holding it in, and I cannot.

I am reminded of the bitterness of Alice Meynell, the late 19th century poet, who from a deeply faithful Christian heart reflected thus on the death of a child:

> We have something to forgive God for. Does that seem a blasphemy? I say that with the little knowledge he has given us and the short sight, we have something to forgive the Creator who makes husband and wife grow one only to smite them in two again, who prodigally overdoes and exaggerates the love in a woman's heart and then forces her to watch her child's long agony. If we saw all we should have nothing to forgive. But he makes us see so little and he must wish us to forgive him . . . We forgive thee our Maker for thy infinite inventiveness in planning the anguish of human life.

Yet Jeremiah also discovers that affliction can somehow lead him to the very heart of God. There are times when, like Dietrich Bonhoeffer, Jeremiah feels that God has deserted him. Bonhoeffer said:

> It is like an invasion from outside, as though evil powers were trying to deprive one of life's dearest treasures.

Jeremiah would have understood that feeling. But he would also have understood the quite remarkable insight of Simone Weil:

The outward results of affliction are nearly always bad. We lie when we try to disguise this. It is in affliction, however, that the splendour of God's mercy shines from its very depths in the heart of its inconsolable bitterness. If still persevering in our love, we fall to the point where we cannot keep back the cry 'My God, why hast thou forsaken me?', if we remain touching at this point without ceasing to love, we end by touching something which is not affliction, but something which is the very love of God.

Is this something we can understand too?

Out of this experience Jeremiah discovers a deeply personal communion with God. He discovers that even though the bond between Judah and God is fractured, as an individual he can still remain close to God. This may seem commonplace to a 20th century Christian, but it was quite a revolutionary experience for people of Jeremiah's time. He was a pioneer. He was paving the way for some of the greatest of the Psalms, for the *Confessions* of St Augustine and St Thomas à Kempis, and for the mystical writing of Lady Julian of Norwich. Perhaps even men like John Wesley and George Fox as well as Dietrich Bonhoeffer owe something to the discovery of personal communion with God in the suffering of Jeremiah.

That communion gives rise to two fine expressions of devotion to God to be found in the very middle of Jeremiah's bitterest feelings. In 17:7-8 and 12-14 the faith of the prophet is spoken with amazing confidence and ends with a moving prayer:

Heal me, O Lord, and I shall be healed; save me and I shall be saved. For you are my praise.

Some reflections

This is one of the few places in the Old Testament where doubt and fear stand side by side with confidence and faith. We see that it is possible for men and women to suffer great difficulties and tragedy, where faith almost disappears, and anger and reproach are on the lips of God-fearing people. Yet in the mercy of God we are preserved from spiritual destruction. God is infinitely more understanding of honest doubt and suffering fear than we sometimes give him credit for.

The prophecy also sheds light on the place of solitude in the spiritual life. The distinguished mathematician and philosopher A. N. Whitehead once said that religion is what a person does with solitariness. There are numerous ways of interpreting this but it certainly implies that moments of solitude are crucial to faith, and there can be no doubt that the most remarkable moments in biblical history alone tend to be in extreme solitude. Jacob at Bethel and Peniel, Moses on Sinai, Christ in the wilderness of temptation are but three outstanding instances. Do we overemphasise the element of fellowship in our thinking about Christian discipleship?

This emphasis on personal religion also affects the way that the religious community, and therefore the Church, has been regarded. Just as being an Israelite made a person one of the people of God and gave him or her a relationship with God through the nation, so national Churches like the Church of England have in the past regarded the Church as 'the nation at prayer'. To be baptised, to communicate according to the rubric and to live a sober moral life, satisfied the demands upon the individual. By contrast, Churches which were 'gathered' consisted of those who had made a personal commitment to Christ and were active in the fellowship of the church as well as in its weekly worship. The older Hebrew tradition was faced by

Jeremiah's assertion that personal commitment and personal faith were the secret of communion with God. In one sense Jeremiah may have been the first great evangelical. For him only a change of heart can make men and women truly fit to be the people of God. And that is part of the subject of our next study.

Questions
1. Jeremiah gave voice to his doubts. Is it possible that doubts are a necessary part of our spiritual growth?

2. Despite both anger and despondency Jeremiah could not give up his calling as a prophet. Is this part of the experience of Christian preachers, teachers and church workers?

3. Try to find some acted parables in the ministry of Jesus. (Try John 13 and Matthew 18:1-4 just for a start.) In what ways are they different from those of Jeremiah?

4. Jeremiah's attitude to his persecutors seems vindictive. Is this an excuse for Christians to be unforgiving?

5. Is it fundamentally true or false that religion is what we do with our solitariness? Look at the practical implications of your answer.

6. Affliction can wreck faith. Explore some ways in which, however, it may actually deepen Christian trust in God. Search your hymn book for some examples.

7. Do you regard the Church as a gathering of committed and active Christians or as the community at worship and prayer? What practical significance has your answer for the way in which the Church is organised and functions?

8. Ask each member of the group to try to bring a hymn, poem, or passage from a diary or journal which seems to express attitudes similar to those of Jeremiah
   a) in doubt
   b) in grief
   c) in communion with God despite adversity.

Chapter 7

Jeremiah (2)
Redemption and Grace

We see deeds done that are so evil, and injuries that are so great, that it seems to us quite impossible that any good can come of them. As we consider these, sorrowfully and mournfully, we cannot relax in the blessed contemplation of God as we ought. This is caused by the fact that our reason is now so blind, base and ignorant that we are unable to know that supreme and marvellous wisdom, might and goodness which belong to the blessed Trinity. This is the meaning of his word 'You will see for yourself that all manner of thing shall be well.' It is as if he were saying: 'Be careful now to believe and trust and in the end you will see it all in its fullness and glory.'

Julian of Norwich, *Revelations of Divine Love*

Passages for study: Jeremiah 31:28-40, 32:6-25 and 37-42.

A commitment of hope

We have already seen how, in two acted parables, Jeremiah warned Jerusalem of its imminent destruction. In chapter 32 he is involved in a similar dramatic sign which offers hope and faith to his people. The purport of it is very much in tune with the hopefulness in adversity voiced by Julian of Norwich in the passage at the head of this study.

To understand this story we need to know something of a custom which was common among ancient and early medieval peoples.

Henry McKeating has explained that under the ancient legal system, it was up to a tribe or clan to provide security for its members. If one was injured they must bring the wrongdoer to justice. If one of their own family was accused they must support him in court. And the nearest kinsman on whom the responsibility principally fell was called 'redeemer' which is the normal translation of the world 'go'el'. The go'el would have to act if a kinsman was about to be sold into slavery to pay a debt or, if he had to sell his land, the go'el would have the opportunity to buy it rather than allow it to pass into the hands of strangers. This system was probably used in Anglo-Saxon England in very early days until the village community took over the responsibility from the tribe or kin.

In the story which begins at 32:6, Jeremiah's cousin, Hanameel is in some difficulty – probably through debt – and as next of kin it is Jeremiah's duty to act as go'el and to redeem the land. With great precision he does so. All the legal formalities are observed and the contracts completed. (v10-11). Then Jeremiah orders his secretary to place the deeds in an earthenware pot and probably to bury them for security, so that they will not be lost in the disorder that will follow the fall of Jerusalem (v12-14).

The incident has a twofold significance. In the first place it points to a much greater redemption which God himself will accomplish. It is likely that the Jews, like most ancient peoples, believed that in the last resort God himself would be the go'el for a man who had neither kindred nor any other possible go'el. Here there is an implied promise in Jeremiah's action that, just as he has redeemed his cousin's land, so God will one day redeem the land of Judah from its conquerors.

Such a hope, when the Chaldeans have already taken possession of the very land which Jeremiah has redeemed, almost seems perverse. Indeed Jeremiah himself appears to be daunted. In a very moving prayer in 32:17-24 he acknowledges God as creator of all things (v17) and praises his love, faithfulness and his justice in his dealings with humankind (v18-19). He remembers all that God has done for Israel (v20-23). But, despite his obedience in loyally redeeming his cousin's land, he appears to question the wisdom of what he has done (v25).

God's answer is gracious. After reminding Jeremiah of the evils which have brought calamity upon Jerusalem, in v37 he promises to gather the people together once more. There will be a new life for them and they will henceforth live in obedience to him. The last verses of the chapter promise a time of renewed stability and social order. This hope is repeated a number of times in the prophecy. It is remarkable in the dire circumstances in which it was written. Yet Jeremiah has, by his act of faith in God's future, purchased a share in that future for his family and committed himself to that hope. It is a potent symbol.

The nature of future hope

The Jews expected a prosperous material future in the providence of God. They expected that the great kingdom of David would be restored under one of David's descendants. It would be a time when they would be faithful to God, and, as a reward, God would punish their enemies. Jeremiah may not have been quite so crudely materialist in his hope, but he would be in a small minority.

We are equally confused about the future. Indeed 21st century people are very short on hope.

In the 19th century it was widely assumed that, just as people had sloughed off abuses like slavery, child labour, a savage and cruel penal system, and had vastly improved the conditions in cities and towns, so education, science and civil goodwill would create a perfect society. Progress was believed to be inevitable. If you have a copy of the *Methodist Hymn Book* and turn to hymn 910 you will find an expression of this hope:

> These things shall be; a loftier race
>> Than e'er the world hath known shall rise,
> With flame of freedom in their souls
>> And light of knowledge in their eyes.

The third verse is even more idealistic:

> Nation with nation, land with land,
>> Inarmed shall live as comrades free;
> In every heart and brain shall throb
>> The pulse of one fraternity.

Perhaps the omission of this hymn from *Hymns & Psalms* is due not simply to the vagueness of its theology, but also to the fact that we no longer believe fervently in progress. Some things appear to improve, but we are much more conscious of human misery as it pleads with us from our television sets in our own homes. The horrors we perpetrate seem more and more terrifyingly inhuman.

Perhaps partly because the mind and heart of man are capable of devising and perpetrating so much evil, some Christians believe that only a final cataclysmic intervention by God can end the evil of the world. Some, indeed, would deny that it is any use trying to improve the human lot. In their view, and they turn to the book of Revelation to prove it, things can only get worse until the day of God dawns.

A third option assumes that good and evil, love and hatred, truth and falsehood, joy and suffering will remain as long as there is life on the planet. The hope of the Christian is a purely personal one in which, after death, the faithful Christian will enjoy in a fuller way the eternal life which he has begun to experience here on earth.

If, however, we retreat into a private faith and abandon completely any deep concern for the future of our people and the planet, we are left with a number of searching questions.

There is a very deep-rooted human instinct which is always bent on securing a better world for its children. Nor is this unchristian. From his prison cell Dietrich Bonhoeffer wrote:

> Is not righteousness and the kingdom of God on earth the focus of everything? . . . It is not with the next world that we are concerned, but this world as created and preserved and made subject to laws and atoned for and made new.

So we cannot retreat from that responsibility for hope without being guilty of indifference to human need and suffering and injustice.

Can we really claim as Christians that the hope of personal blessedness is sufficient to justify the agonies and aspirations of long centuries of human life? What people have lived and died for, seeking the deliverance of their fellows from oppression, desperate necessity and pain, can surely not be vindicated by less than the kingdom of God.

God and human responsibility
It was perhaps to be expected that Jeremiah, whose sense of personal communion with God was so acute, should

proclaim a belief in personal responsibility which also was highly individual and revolutionary.

The promise of a new and restored Israel in 31:28f declares that 'all shall die for their own sins' (v30). What Jeremiah is saying is that every person has responsibility for their own sins. He takes exception to the accepted belief that the children suffer for the sins of their fathers, that each generation is already under threat of suffering because of the errors and sins of its ancestors. In the words of v29, 'The parents have eaten sour grapes, and the children's teeth are set on edge.' This he did not believe.

In this he is also challenging the doctrine contained in the Ten Commandments (Exodus 20:5) which lays down that God does punish the children for their father's sins.

The idea that we have absolute responsibility for our own sins is a Christian belief. But it was novel in Jeremiah's day. It was an important step forward in the moral development of humankind because it linked the possibility of personal communion with God to the possibility that an individual, by his wrongdoing, might turn away from God. The belief that God, through the life, death and resurrection of Jesus, has reconciled us as individuals to himself would have been impossible without that first step.

But Jeremiah overstates the point and fails to see the deep truth which lies in the traditional belief.

One generation cannot be insulated from the mistakes and wrongdoing of its predecessors. The mistrust, aggressive tempers and sheer foolishness which provoked the First World War had effects on the lives of fatherless children in the 1920s and 1930s which must have affected their moral development. And the selfishness of older rulers in that same period cost more and more lives in the Second World War. Examples could be multiplied from every century of our history.

The same principle can be seen at work in the more private sphere. A child whose behaviour is subject to poor role models in the home has much leeway to make up in adolescence. Equally if the child is taught that kindness and compassion are weak and unmanly, and if it is starved of parental love, then he or she will have the greatest difficulty in achieving loving relationships. It is impossible to divorce a child's moral development from its inheritance and moral environment.

Jeremiah also fails to recognise the responsibility which we have for the pressures which afflict others. Our fears, our aspirations, our prejudices combine with others to create an unjust or ill-directed society. We need to be aware of this as well as to accept our responsibility for our own obvious sins.

The new covenant
In 17:9 Jeremiah points out that the source of evil is in the human heart because 'the heart is devious above all else; it is perverse'. In 4:14 he exhorts the people 'to wash your heart clean of wickedness so that you may be saved'. Those verses could easily have come from the New Testament, and indeed Jeremiah comes very close to preaching a gospel.

That preaching centres round a New Covenant. The religion of the Old Testament was based on a Covenant faith. It was based on the belief that God had called Israel to be his special people and had bound himself to them by promises not unlike the promises of the covenant of marriage. On their side the Israelites had vowed themselves to be faithful to their God. This covenant was broken by the Israelites (31:32). Now there will be a new covenant. Men and women henceforth will not obey the laws of God from fear or custom or convention, but because they love God's law and enjoy obeying him. They will come to love goodness. In the words of Jeremiah, God will have written the law on their hearts (31:33). An inner revolution will have taken place.

When a Christian preacher exhorts people to repent, promises God's forgiveness and calls them to a faith in Christ which will mean a new and changed life, he is echoing Jeremiah's promise of a radical change of heart. And it is significant that Jesus himself at the Last Supper referred to his blood as the seal upon the New Covenant between God and those who accepted Christ. He was inaugurating by his death the New Covenant of which Jeremiah had spoken.

We think of that gift as very personal – a means of individual salvation. Jeremiah thought that the individual transformation would change the whole life of the nation, and that idea has also been current in the Christian Church. In the 1940s, when people were anticipating the post-war period with a mixture of hope and apprehension, preachers would often speak of the necessity of changing the human heart as the only way of changing the world. A favourite illustration was a jigsaw puzzle which had the figure of a man on one side and a map of the world on the other. If you got the figure of the man right, then automatically you got the map right. 'A change of heart changes the world,' said the preacher, and Jeremiah would have concurred.

I thought then that this was very naïve and simplistic. I still do.

It is true that in subtle ways the change of personal values and attitudes in a substantial minority of people can profoundly affect the national life. But there are very powerful influences at work in modern society, through the media in particular, which it is very difficult to shake off. We are never quite so free in our personal decisions as we like to think.

Moreover it is very easy to take refuge in our own personal religious experience which keeps us close to Christ, and do little about the evils and injustices which afflict our fellows, because we think the only way to change things is to change the human heart, that it can only be done by the preacher and not the reformer.

The grace of God brings us into a greater understanding of God's ways, enables us to see the world through his eyes rather than our own and so offers us a counterpoint to the persuasive influences of a materialist culture. That is where Jeremiah still speaks to us.

Questions
1. In what ways is the Christian, like Jeremiah, committed to hope? Can a Christian ever be an unredeemed pessimist?

2. Which of the three expressions of hope for the future seems most justified by the Christian faith?

3. Is there a Christian responsibility for the welfare of the next generation? How can it be fulfilled?

4. Herbert Butterfield once said that there are evils for which no one is directly responsible, but which are the responsibility of every person in the society in which they exist. For instance, we may be responsible for wrongs done by a Trades Union, or a political party of which we are members, or a company of which we are shareholders. Discuss this problem.

5. What difference should our Christian discipleship make to our values?

6. 'Change the person and change the world.' Is it true?

7. Is it possible to reconcile the idea that we are responsible for our own wrongdoing with the recognition that character can be distorted by environment and heredity which are outside our control?

Chapter 8

The Second Isaiah
(1) God in History and Providence

Faith in providence is another aspect of that awareness of God as personal which, we have maintained, lies somewhere at the root of all man's religious history.

H. H. Farmer, *The World and God*

Passage for study: Isaiah 40:1-11

These verses are inseparably associated with Handel's *Messiah* for which they provide a section of the libretto. So we are apt to think of it simply as a prophecy of the coming of the Messiah. This handicaps our understanding because there is an older Jewish understanding of the passage which is just as relevant for the Christian. All the passages we shall be studying from this prophecy are written as poetry in the original Hebrew, and very beautiful poetry at that.

The circumstances in which the prophecy was made are not in doubt. In 586BC Jerusalem was sacked by the Chaldeans, who carried away the upper classes of the Jewish population into slavery, leaving a ruined, undefended city and an impoverished, dispirited and leaderless population. As for those who were taken into exile, many found it more congenial to accept and even enjoy the way of life of their conquerors. They intermarried and practised the religion of Babylon. Only a remnant remained true to their God.

Who was the prophet?
We do not know the identity of this poet-prophet who wrote chapters 40 to 55 of the prophecy of Isaiah. He was

an outstanding poet and a man of penetrating spiritual insight. It seems likely that he lived around 550BC at a time when Cyrus, the king of Persia, threatened and eventually conquered the Chaldeans. Cyrus is actually mentioned in the prophecy (Isaiah 44:28 and 45:1).

Where the prophet lived is more doubtful. Some scholars believe that he was in Babylon. Others think he may have lived in a Jewish colony in Egypt. Adolphe Lods, however, has pointed out that since he depicts Babylonians chopping down trees to make idols it is hardly likely that he was familiar with Babylon, which was largely bereft of trees. Lods thinks that the prophet lived in either the region of Tyre and Sidon, or in Palestine. He frequently mentions the cedars of Lebanon, which may be a clue to his whereabouts.

His announcement is addressed both to the exiles and those disheartened spirits around Jerusalem. It is an impassioned utterance.

The Good News
The message is a confident answer to the doubts which have weakened his people. They have been unable to escape two insistent questions. They have been taught that their God was just. If so, why have they endured such suffering? They had been taught that, from the days of Abraham, Israel have been chosen by God as his people. If so, why has he cast them off and allowed them to be conquered by the Chaldeans?

The good tidings which burst forth in the very first verse are almost equivalent to a gospel. To men and women who have questioned the very foundations of their faith comes the announcement that they are forgiven. They have suffered for their sins but they have endured more than enough for all their wrongdoing (v1-2). God is righteous and just and his pardon will confirm the fact. They have not been cast off and so for the second time in the history of Israel, God himself will lead his people out of captivity across the desert back to their homeland, just as he had led them out of Egypt into Canaan in the time of Moses (v3-5).

The herald is a lonely voice 'crying in the wilderness' (v3). No one can believe that the wonder of the Exodus from Egypt under Moses will be repeated, that the forbidding mountains will be levelled and the treacherous wadis filled in, that the triumphant procession of God's people, led by their God in person, will return to Jerusalem (v4). The people have given way to a fatalistic pessimism. Everything is 'here today and gone tomorrow' and there is no meaning or value in life (v6-7). Yet the lonely voice retorts: 'The grass withers, the flower fades; but the word of our God will stand for ever' (v8).

The joyful announcement reaches a crescendo in verses 9-11. Not just the exiles but the dispirited inhabitants of Jerusalem now hear the Good News as it comes from Mount Zion itself, from the very hill upon which the God of Israel has caused his presence to dwell. He is still in their midst and he will be their shepherd, caring for them with an exquisite gentleness and tenderness. Once more he will be the true king of his people as in the former days, and Jerusalem will be the city of God.

This announcement of a new Exodus is repeated again and again in the prophecy (eg. 41:18-20 and 42:15-16). And at the end of chapter 44 and the beginning of chapter 45 it is made clear that the prophet envisages that when Cyrus of Persia conquers the Chaldeans, the Persian king will be God's servant in setting the Jews free and facilitating their return to Jerusalem. The book of Nehemiah shows clearly how Cyrus did in fact liberate the Jews and enable them to return and to begin rebuilding Jerusalem. So the prophecy was to that extent fulfilled.

The Jews and providence

The proclamation of Good News raises questions about the way the prophet looked at the history of his people, and the manner in which his words were interpreted.

The central place of Cyrus in the Good News is, first of all, unexpected. That Isaiah should have believed that God would raise up a new and charismatic leader for his people would not surprise the Jews. After all, the prophet's namesake centuries earlier had spoken of such a great leader, who would be a descendant of David (Isaiah 9:6-7 and 11:1-16). But although Cyrus was a just and upright prince, he did not worship Israel's God, nor was he one of God's people. Nor, so far as we can judge, was he conscious of being a specially appointed servant of the Lord. Yet he fulfilled God's purpose. How could this happen?

The answer lies in the prophet's faith in the supreme power and wisdom of God. In the next study we shall see that, for the prophet, God is the creator of the ends of the earth controlling not simply his own people, but the nations of the earth. It is he who will lead his people, and in his hands even the most powerful of princes must be a subservient agent. Nations are, after all, 'a drop from a bucket' and 'dust on the scales' (40:15). Such is the world panorama which the prophet's vision embraces. None of his great predecessors like Amos or Hosea, or even Jeremiah, would have received such a vision. But it is the vision of the poet-prophet which ultimately provides the backcloth for the worldwide Church, the vision of Paul and the subject of Luke's great writings.

That raises another related question. If God sits on the throne of the universe how can Israel, this insignificant little people, never mentioned in the chronicles of the ancient world, be God's chosen people? The prophet had an answer which we shall find in the next two studies, but for the moment we need to notice that his world-embracing vision continued to be in conflict with the narrow prejudice of those Jews who were hostile to the Gentiles well beyond the time of Christ.

Henry McKeating has drawn attention to a third question. The prophet is confident that the new Jerusalem will be the ideal city of God. His poetic vision and his idealism will not tolerate the thought of anything less. But, as McKeating points out, the very colourful language made the actual fulfilment something of a let-down. Indeed the future would be a time of disheartening struggle to rebuild not only the city, but the religious life of the people. Neighbours were unfriendly, resources were limited and the people not always equal to the high demands of their faith. Only once were the Jews an independent people, and that was briefly under the Maccabees. Suffering was to be their lot in the future as it had been in the past.

So it is not surprising that the faithful began to reinterpret the Good News to mean that at the end of the ages, when God recreated the world, the prophet's dream would be fulfilled. And similarly in the first century the followers of Jesus took the passage to refer to the good news of the gospel. The lonely voice was the voice of John the Baptist and his 'news' the imminent coming of Christ. The new age which the Christians believed had dawned was for them the fulfilment of the prophet's dream.

Some reflections

This wonderful picture of an active God has not sat easily beside the man-centred thinking of the last 500 years.

Medieval Christians still believed in an active God, though they believed that his activity was channelled by Holy Church. But by the late 17th century it was commonly accepted that God was a remote and disinterested First Cause who had so fashioned the universe that it could get along without him. If people lived according to the laws of nature they would not need the active presence of God. The world was theirs and in it their intellect, inventiveness and creative talents could flourish.

The optimistic minds of the 18th century put their faith in reason rather than in God, and asserted that there was no problem which calm reasoning could not ultimately solve. Scientific progress and industrial prosperity together with the development of democratic societies seemed to confirm the optimism.

It was only when, in the 20th century, it became increasingly obvious that world problems and personal problems alike are often intractable that hope became corroded. Utopia is now dismissed as a baseless dream and optimism is in short supply.

But without any widespread faith in a living God the resources for a different kind of hope seem lacking. Nothing illustrates this more surely than the rapid dissolution of the hope which emerged with the revolutions in Eastern Europe in 1989. The *annus mirabilis* has been followed by grim hopelessness, by the revival of bitter nationalism, and by decadence and crime. There was nothing, other than Western greed, to fill the vacuum.

A minority of Christians today find it impossible to believe in a personal God, and outside the organised Church, faith is rarely found. The question is whether that faith can be recovered and with it a belief in a future which is within God's purpose.

It also involves believing in providence. That too defeats the faith of many. H. H. Farmer once declared that a belief in providence was essential to a healthy faith. In his book, *The World and God,* he pointed out that it is where the twin aspects of evil confront us in the form of suffering and sin that we are driven to look for the presence of a Divine providence.

It is not that human beings react adversely to hardship and pain. They actually invite them by climbing Everest or running marathons. But in Farmer's words:

> They become a problem precisely at the point where they seem no longer to serve the high ends of zestful endeavour and a strong personal life, but rather to run counter to them; that is to say where they seem to negate human personality rather than minister to it.

Calamities, the suffering of those we love, the apparent success of those who live evil lives, all challenge our sense of spiritual well-being. Sometimes it almost seems as if love itself is the enemy of our faith. In the face of our doubts we long for the intervention of providence.

But can it happen? Farmer has suggested that, for the Christian, one old Bible story may encapsulate the truth. It is the story of how Joseph, having risen from slavery to high authority in Egypt, is reunited with his brothers and his father. At his father's death the brothers fear that

Joseph will be avenged upon them because they sold him into slavery. Joseph replies:

> Even though you intended to do harm to me, God intended it for good, in order to preserve a numerous people, as he is doing today.
>
> Genesis 50:20

Farmer asks where providence lies in that situation? Could it be that God had engineered the whole thing, inspiring the brothers with evil desires, inspiring the passion of Potiphar's wife, the crimes and dreams of court officials and so forth? Wisely Farmer rejects such a naïve solution and suggests that there could be an alternative. Very simply, God responded to events and experiences caused by human jealousy, sexual passion and dishonesty and by his presence with Joseph gave him those qualities which enabled him to be a saving agent in the time of disastrous famine. Evil did not have its own way because providence ruled the heart and mind of Joseph.

There is a pointer here to a principle which finds its supreme expression on the cross. A crucifixion, brought about by human sin, became an act of divine grace, because God ruled in the heart and mind of Christ. Perhaps there is here a sign that, where God does rule hearts and minds, there is no need to despair of God's future. I suspect that the poet-prophet of the Exile would have concurred.

Which brings us back to where we began. In the story of Joseph, in the Good News of the poet-prophet, and in the cross, God's providential activity involves forgiveness, setting men free from the imprisonment of past misdeeds, perhaps setting the world free from its past crimes and blind furies. Is this ultimately where providence is still to be recognised, in the grace that does not allow us to destroy ourselves and that allows the world to wake up to moments when a new dawn brings new hope? I would like to think that the optimism of the poet-prophet still is valid today.

Questions

1. Farmer suggests that men and women do not object to hardship and even suffering unless it is destructive of what is valuable in their lives. Do you agree?

2. What dangers lie in a situation where as individuals or communities people have lost hope?

3. 'I believe that in spite of the recent triumphs of science, men haven't changed much in the last 2,000 years; and in consequence we must learn from history. History is ourselves.' (Kenneth Clark) Is this a true summary of our human situation or is there another, nearer to the truth?

4. Do you think it is possible for God to use people without their conscious co-operation?

5. Do you believe that our lives are governed by providence? If so, what light does Farmer throw on its operation?

6. Look at the closing paragraph of this study. Do you think that grace is always the last word of God's providence in the world?

7. Is it through his own suffering and that of dedicated human beings that God is able to act in the world?

8. A critic might say that if there is a God the universe is too vast and our planet and ourselves too small for him to have a personal concern for us. Try to convince him otherwise.

Chapter 9

The Second Isaiah
(2) God in Nature

I saw Eternity the other night
Like a great Ring of pure and endless light,
　　All calm as it was bright.
And round beneath it, Time, in hours, days, years,
　　Driven by the spheres,
Like a vast shadow moved, in which the world
　　And all her train were hurled.

Henry Vaughan

Passage for study: Isaiah 40:12-31

The conditions of the exile

From the joyful assurance of the Herald Voice, the prophet turns his attention to his hearers. The contrast is reminiscent of that between the scene on the Mount of Transfiguration and the frustration of the disciples in the valley below when they fail to heal the epileptic boy (Mark 9).

For one reason or another his hearers are sceptical. It is not so much that they are suffering physical privation as that their faith is severely undermined. Their God is the God of Zion, of the hills and rich fertile countryside, of the people of Israel. How can such a God be worshipped in the endless plain, in the sophisticated city, away from Zion? 'How can we sing the songs of Zion in a strange land?' is their cry. If they are in Babylon, then they can only worship the gods of Babylon.

It is easy to say that they were spiritually immature, but we should not forget that a great deal of human religion today is just as closely bound up with family ties, with a particular church, with a style of worship and fellowship, even with a particular local community. Let work or other ambitions carry people away to some entirely different situation and their faith can be threatened, even disappear. John Oman once said that Wapping Quay was reputedly the most religious place in Britain because it was where emigrants left their religion behind. Perhaps the collapse of community and the increased movement of population in Britain may be a cause of reduced church attendance, as well as the inability of men and women to accept the Christian faith.

The Lord our God is one Lord

There were two classes of people to whom the prophet addressed his remonstrance. There were those who had deserted the God of Israel and worshipped the Babylonian gods. There were also those who, though still loyal to Yahweh, were in the depths of despair from which even the prophet's good news could not rouse them. The basic message to both is the same, though the implications are different.

The prophet paints a word picture of a God whose works can be seen by people of every nation, wherever they are. They have only to lift up their eyes and look at the heavens, heavens which are as visible in Palestine as they are in Babylon (v26). Their God is the Creator of all things and can be worshipped in Babylon as easily as in Zion. The image of this Creator is awesome. In his presence human ingenuity is but a poor reflection (v12-14 and v22). The very nations are like the dust on a scale after the weighing is complete (v15). The great rulers of the earth exist simply by permission of the Creator God (v23-24) and they can be overthrown by God at a moment's notice. In fact the rulers of Babylon may look impressive but they are at the mercy of a power besides whom they are as nothing.

It is a remarkable poetic vision besides which only perhaps Psalm 8 can stand comparison. Yet it is born in the prophet's mind not from his people's tradition, but from inspiration in response to his people's need. Only by such a vision could they become aware that the God of Zion, whose people they are, is the one God of all the earth.

There is some disagreement among scholars as to how soon the realisation that there was but one God who was the Creator of all things dawned on Israel. There are signs that, until the Exile, there was a general feeling that Yahweh was the greatest of Gods, but that the gods of other peoples were real enough. Notice, for instance, Psalm 95:3:

> For the Lord is a great God, and a great King
> above all gods.

But it may well be that, as early as the Exodus, a great spirit, like Moses, had grasped the truth which it took others hundreds of years to accept. The first two chapters of Amos suggest that God is the judge of other peoples besides Israel and in Amos 5:8 there is a picture of God as Creator which has a rare beauty.

But it is our poet-prophet who for the first time makes a clear proclamation that the God of Israel is the Creator of all things. It is a moment of great significance in the history of our faith.

The New Testament takes this belief for granted as Christians do today. But there are few references to the natural world which God has created. Jesus himself paints a very intimate picture of a God who cares even for sparrows, and of the security we have in trusting him. Paul, in 2 Corinthians 6, speaks of the God who caused light to shine out of darkness, and in Romans 8:22 refers to creation as 'groaning'. In Ephesians 1:10 there is an anticipation of the time when the whole Creation will be perfected. But there is no great vision of the Creator. The New Testament is centred on Christ the Redeemer.

The Russian theologian, Nicholai Berdyaev, has pointed out that Christian teaching has steered the attention of its people from nature because it was believed that Christian discipline meant that the natural desires and appetites of humankind had to be suppressed. Religions which made much of nature tended to elevate natural man, instead of subjecting him to discipline. In Berdyaev's own words:

> Christianity had effected man's deliverance from the terror and slavery of nature; but in order to achieve this it had been obliged to declare an uncompromising, passionate and heroic war on the natural elements both within and outside man, an ascetic war illustrated by the astounding lives of the saints.

It was not until the 17th century that nature was allowed to resume a central place in the human imagination. For example, Rubens was the first of a great line of landscape painters who revealed the light and the enormous expanse of the natural world and the relative smallness of the human figure. As a Christian Rubens was both humbled and consoled, but it was easy for later artists to lose the background of faith, and to see no further than the beauty of nature, or, as in the case of the French painter Delacroix, to be stimulated by its cruelty and wildness.

The Romantic poets like Wordsworth took up the same theme with varying degrees of religious faith, or lack of it.

Once more nature became a source of joy, refreshment and peace in a way that the Christian Church had rarely envisaged. This may seem surprising to men and women for whom nature is a consolation and a part of their faith. They at any rate will find a spiritual comrade in our poet-prophet.

The challenge to idolatry
The prophet's first words are to those who have adopted the Babylonian religion. Not only in this chapter but again and again in the prophecy the writer pours scorn on idols. In 41:21-29 he challenges the idols themselves to a contest, almost reminiscent of Elijah's contest with the prophets of Baal on Mount Carmel. They are to bring their predictions for the future to see if they have the gift of prophecy. But of course (41:28) they cannot answer even a word. Then, with searing sarcasm, in 44:15 he pictures the devotee of idols using one part of a tree to bake his bread and to warm himself and the rest to make an idol. And in the present passage (40:18-20) he contrasts the great Creator with the empty images of Babylon. Surely no self-respecting Israelite can be so deluded as to worship them!

Protestant Christianity has historically been greatly offended by the use of figures of Christ in churches and perhaps has accepted much more reprehensible forms of inferior worship too easily. The real idolatry consists in giving to another person or object the central place in life which is rightly God's. Extreme forms of hero worship, uncritical loyalty to fallible politicians and leaders, the pursuit of wealth or ambition with an increasingly self-absorbed ruthlessness: these are the real idolatries of our time. They are damaging to society and to the perpetrators as they are ridiculous. Our poet-prophet still merits a hearing from us today.

The great renewal

How different are the prophet's warm and comforting words to the discouraged and despairing few. Verses 26-31 are some of the richest in the Old Testament. The Creator God, who renews the life of nature (v26), will renew the life of his people. The physical symbols here clearly have a spiritual significance. They who wait on God (v31) shall be renewed with truly revolutionary results.

George Adam Smith a century ago pointed out how the prophet reverses the normal course of human behaviour. In our first flush of enthusiasm we feel we could easily fly. In the event we begin by running until, out of breath, we are reduced to walking at a poor stumbling rate. It is not long before we fling ourselves down, exhausted. Our prophet paints a picture of men and women empowered by God who are borne up by ideals that seem to have wings, who run their race of life without wearying, and who go through the punishing weariness of everyday duties, walking without fainting – the most stringent test of spiritual endurance. Here is assurance for the despairing exiles if they will but wait upon God.

Some reflections

We are used to regarding nature as full of scenes of great majesty and beauty in which we find refreshment and recuperation. We do not always see that within nature are powers of renewal that point us to a renewing God as surely as they did the prophet. How often our own bodies find within themselves the sources of healing! How regularly sleep fits us once more for the demands of the day! How wonderfully plants provide for fertilisation by attracting insects to act as their agents! And season follows season without fail so that only an exceptional divergence from normal weather draws our attention to the process. The prophet had placed his finger unerringly on the truth.

Nor does nature provide the only stage for this endless drama. History itself shows moments of unexpected renewal. Great leaders arise who challenge dying ideals and bring to ordinary people a cleansing of the spirit, deliverance from selfishness, and a new readiness to care for their nation, their community and their neighbours. The deliverance is rarely enduring but life is transformed despite that loss. It will need another similar moment to renew what has been once more ruined by selfishness and scepticism.

Our own time exhibits both exciting renewal and fading ideals. The impulse which has revolutionised the relationships between the Christian Churches in Britain owes its origins to Christian leaders who quietly and persistently learned to respect each others' traditions long before the ordinary worshipping Christian looked beyond his own church walls. The changes in the last 40 years have been almost unbelievable. We are not free from either prejudice or misunderstanding and it may be that there will be severe setbacks before us. But the setting for Christian conversations will never be the same again.

Twenty years ago the most optimistic European liberal would not have believed it possible that Nelson Mandela would ever become President of South Africa. Wind of change there may have been, but the revolutionary renewal of South Africa seemed a pipe dream. Here again there have been setbacks, but the possibilities for renewal have been radically increased. The same could be said of the Church in China, where, against all the odds, a quietly persisting Christian community was suddenly exposed to view after nearly 30 years underground.

What nature and events thus reveal is seen also in the life of Jesus himself. He healed diseased bodies, restored sight and hearing and speech, gave the crippled a new ability to walk. He restored the leper and the demoniac to their families and to their place in the community. His pardon renewed the freedom of the spirit for those who were set free. The pattern delineated by the poet-prophet of the Exile was fulfilled in Galilee.

A postscript

There is a final challenge to us in v31. We too have youthful ideals, often impatient and impractical. We would fly too. In the service of those ideals we run as long as our spiritual stamina lasts and as long as disillusionment does not cloud our vision. But perhaps most testing of all we find that ideals demand a daily loyalty, a sometimes wearisome repetition of rather humble duties, an exchange of glorious excitement for very humdrum chores. And we faint.

The truth is, however, that God renews our ideals even while experience renders them more practical. He inspires and enables us to bring enthusiasm to our discipleship. His strength enables us to 'walk and not faint'.

One of the most moving stories in the history of British Christianity is that of Mary Jones, the Welsh girl who, having painfully saved money that she had earned at some sacrifice, walked 25 miles in her bare feet over wild unpaved tracks, carrying her shoes in order that at the end after walk, they might still grace her feet. Her destination was Bala where she hoped to be able to purchase a Bible in Welsh. Through her faithfulness the Bible Society was moved to extend its work of taking the Bible to all who could read in whatever language. Perhaps it is that God renews men and women and restores the life of our world most of all through people like Mary Jones, who have learned to walk and not faint.

Questions

1. In some parts of Europe today religious enmities have helped to embitter even further communal strife. Is this inevitable where religion becomes almost tribal?

2. If we did not possess a) the Old Testament b) the knowledge of God in Christ, what could we learn from nature about God? Would it lead us to a good life?

3. What evidence of renewal do you find a) in nature b) in human affairs? What significance has your answer for your Christian faith?

4. We have spoken of the way in which ideals and our devotion to our beliefs fail us. Think around some of the reasons why this happens and how the failure can be remedied.

5. Which is most necessary – the refurbishing of ideals, the renewal of enthusiasm, or the ability to accept the everyday tediousness of loyal discipleship?

6. Do you think that the Church was mistaken in turning the eyes of Christians away from nature? What resource do you find in nature?

7. The artist Eric Gill once said that the life of a city can be just as spiritually sustaining as the countryside. Do you agree?

8. Compare the attitude to nature in Wordsworth's 'Lines composed a few miles above Tintern Abbey' with the attitude to nature in the Old Testament – for instance, in our present passage and in Psalms 8 and 19.

Chapter 10

The Second Isaiah
(3) The Chosen Servant

Israel was sure of her election, not because some daring thinker hit on the idea and taught it to his disciples, until it spread through the nation, but because she passed through a concrete experience, that has no meaning apart from such an explanation.

H. H. Rowley, *The Rediscovery of the Old Testament*

Passage for study: Isaiah 42:1-7

The Servant Songs
This is the first of four so-called songs (the others being 49:1-6, 50:4-9 and 52:13-53:12) which have quite a distinctive tone and message. So distinctive indeed are these poems that many scholars have decided that they were not written by our poet-prophet. Recently, however, the weight of opinion has come to accept that they are his work.

Entire volumes have been written about these four passages alone. All I can do before considering this first passage is to offer some brief comments on the passages generally.

All the passages are concerned with a figure who is called the Servant of the Lord. He is unidentified. It is uncertain whether he is an actual person or an ideal figure, whether he is the people of Israel personified, or an individual, and whether he is a figure from the past, the prophet himself, or a Messianic figure for the future.

First there are those like G. Adam Smith and Adolphe Lods who think that the prophet is reflecting on the undoubted sufferings of the Jewish people, and seeking to give his people an assurance that those sufferings are not outside the purpose of God. So they believe that the Servant is Israel.

Smith and Lods remind us that Israel had always been the chosen of God (42:1) and they believe that God is here promising that through her sufferings she will bring God's light to the Gentiles (49:6) and also that many will be healed (53:5).

Although this is an attractive idea it trips up over the fact that the Servant is described as meek and submissive (2:2-3 and 53:7-8) and without sin (53:9) which is hardly an appropriate description of the biblical history of the Jews. Moreover in 49:4-9 the Servant is spoken of quite separately from the Jewish people.

Some scholars think that the prophet is describing the sufferings, not of the whole people, but of the remnant who were loyal to their God and this is easier to accept.

Others feel that the Servant is so clearly described that the poet-prophet must have been sketching from life, and they have found models in the Old Testament. Moses has been suggested. So, because of his great sufferings, has Joseph, and nearer to the prophet's own time, Jeremiah. Such attempts to identify the Servant seem justified by chapter 53, where the Servant is described as a figure from the past, and the past tense is used. But, of course, you will find that the other three passages all project into the future. So we are back to square one!

I believe that Henry McKeating has provided the most acceptable explanation. He suggests that the prophet is thinking of an ideal Servant of God and in choosing his model is not very consistent. Sometimes he thinks of the sufferings of his people, sometimes of men like Jeremiah. Sometimes, perhaps, he even reflects on his own suffering. But always he is looking hopefully to an ideal Servant in the future who will fulfil all his hopes of God's purposes. The explanation does not entirely fit the facts, particularly in respect of chapter 53, but it is subject to less objections than most other theories.

The Chosen One of God, his character and destiny

In the first place the Servant is described as the Chosen One of God, the elect. He is gifted with the Spirit of God and his task is to be the agent of justice, not simply for the Jews, but for all humankind.

But this is no stern judge but a person of meek bearing. He does not scream or shout, or call attention to himself in public places (v2). Even though he is a judge he acts with compassion, patience and forbearance. He will recognise and allow for the weakness of men and women, knowing that, though their best qualities are almost destroyed by idolatry and sin, they still have the bruised reed of human virtue and the flickering flame which is a dim awareness of God (v3).

In this task he will not fail until justice is secured in the earth and the most distant islands come to recognise his law (v4). T. H. Robinson has pointed out that the character and the task belong together:

> His tenderness was that of strength and not that of weakness. His light was always clear and pure; his tone was always rich and full. For his aim was to establish righteousness and true righteousness can be

established in the last resort only by means which have no element of violence in them.

All this is possible because the Spirit which possesses him is that of the great Creator who is described in chapter 40. He will hold the Servant and preserve him and send him to the people as a covenant. As we saw in our study of Jeremiah, covenant involves a sacred promise, similar to, for instance, the promises made at marriage. To say that a person is 'a covenant' means that the person becomes a living assurance of God's grace and faithfulness. So when the prophet assures his people of God's faithfulness he is a token of God's goodwill towards his own people and towards the Gentiles, a promise that his justice will be secured (5-6). So the spiritual blindness which has hidden God's ways will be dispersed, and the slavery to evil, which has been so destructive, broken down. The people will be set free (v7).

It is not surprising that the early Church saw here the model for the work of Jesus. Look for a moment at Luke 3:22 where Jesus is spoken of as the one in whom God is well pleased. Then read Luke 4:14-30 and you will quickly recognise the Spirit-filled Servant (4:14 and 18), and the worldwide purpose (4:18 and 25-27).

Some reflections
There are three topics which the passage highlights – the question of calling or vocation, the importance of justice, and the relationship between the service of God and of humanity.

The calling
The idea that both the people of Israel and the prophets were chosen and called by God is very familiar in the Old Testament, as we have noticed already in our study of the prophecy of Hosea.

The national vocation is often noticed in the Psalms. Psalm 33:12 pronounces:

Happy is the nation whose God is the Lord, the people whom he has chosen as his heritage.

Psalm 89:3 speaks of God having a covenant with his chosen people, and Psalm 105:6 addresses Israel as God's chosen.

The same strong sense of being called is often the experience of individuals. Moses' call on Sinai (Exodus 3), Isaiah's call in the Temple (Isaiah 6), Amos taken from his work as a gatherer of sycamore fruit (Amos 7:14) and a trembling Jeremiah confronted by God when he is only a boy (Jeremiah 1:4-10) all confirm this sense of being chosen.

There can be no doubt that the belief that they are the chosen people of God has been of immense spiritual strength to the Jewish people through the terrifying sufferings which have been their history.

The idea of election is, of course, to be found in the New Testament too. Paul believed very intensely in his own high calling as an apostle to the Gentiles and he addresses the Christians to whom he writes as equally chosen by God for his own purposes (1 Corinthians 1:1-2 and Romans 1:1-7). The epistle of Peter sounds the same note (1 Peter 1:1-2). It is not surprising, therefore, that at times in the subsequent history of the Church, groups of Christians have also evinced a strong belief that they are 'elect'. This was particularly true of the Calvinists of the 16th and 17th centuries.

There can be no doubt that some of the most dedicated and effective Christian witness has sprung from this strong sense of being chosen. John Wesley in his evangelism, William Wilberfore in his untiring devotion to the cause of the slaves, William Booth in his ministry to the poor and outcast are but relatively modern examples. But where Christians see themselves as being chosen for some superior favour and contrast their own elevated spiritual condition with those whom they deem God to have rejected, then there can emerge a quite unChristian arrogance.

Men and women are called not to privilege but to service. When that is understood there can be no arrogance, only deep humility, which is the bearing of the Servant in this passage. His character is one of insight, sensitivity and compassion.

How we recognise true vocation varies with the person. One sure evidence, however, is the presence of gifts and graces which are enabling for the task. A gift of genuine rapport with children, the ability to explain carefully and to get an enthusiastic response may tell a man or woman that they are being called to teach. Sometimes a particular gift seems outstanding in a person otherwise not particularly talented. I remember a girl whose academic limitations seemed likely to defeat her sense of vocation to become a nurse. Yet her quality of patience and ability to calm and reassure people in trouble proved to those who watched her that the vocation was truly hers. Whether such calling is from God will be debated by those who would confine God's calling to church members. I wonder.

God's justice
Our passage speaks of the Servant securing justice in the world (v4). A people like the Jews who were very conscious of having suffered injustice were eager to find evidence that God was concerned for justice. But neither in

the ancient world outside Israel, nor in the modern world is that widely believed.

The Greeks like Plato and Aristotle believed that for people to play a full part in the life of their city was to enjoy the highest possible justice. The idea of individual rights was quite foreign to them. They would have been puzzled that people should defend their right to privacy, for instance, or the right to the exercise their own religious beliefs.

Justice in the West since the 16th century has been chiefly concerned with the protection of social peace and law and order on the one hand, and of the life and property of the individual on the other.

Sometimes, however, it has simply become the expression of public opinion and where that occurs justice is often only rough justice. In *The Merchant of Venice*, Shakespeare depicts a court of justice where racial prejudice defeats justice, and in *Measure for Measure* justice is the will of a would-be tyrant.

The law can also express the desire of a community for vengeance against offenders rather than a calm and considered judicial verdict. It is one of the anxieties that sensitive Christians must often feel today when, as too frequently happens, with hindsight the community realises that gross injustice has been done.

Hebrew justice stands as an example which we can ill afford to neglect. In the Old Testament, justice is the righteous will of God. It is totally incorruptible and nothing that human frailty can do can in any way impair it.

As we have already noticed, the Jews believed first of all that in the Torah, they had the Law. If they obeyed the

Law in its entirety then they would fulfil the will of God and justice would be secured. If there were difficulties either in understanding what the Law demanded or applying it in special circumstances, the rabbis would interpret and those interpretations were collected as the traditions which Jesus refers to in Mark 7:5.

They also believed that God did intervene where injustice had been done. The punishment of Ahab and Jezebel when they had brought about the death of Naboth by false accusations in order to grab his land, was a sign that God's justice was not to be mocked.

For us the important thing is that justice was not merely an expression of political expediency, public opinion or even political philosophy. It was an aspect of the will of God. Perhaps we need to remember that.

Christian thinking has taken that a little further. God's justice is as individual as his redemptive love. His justice is not only incorruptible, but it is backed by his total understanding of our weaknesses, the pressures that distort us, the injustices we may ourselves have suffered, and so far from being in contrast to his love, it expresses that love in action. How might human justice today be more sensitive if we reflected more on the justice of God?

The love of God and the love of our neighbour

Adam G. Smith, commenting on this passage, has pointed out that the Jews always placed the service of God and obedience to his Law as the primary human obligation. It was not that duty to the neighbour was less important, as the central chapters of Deuteronomy make clear, but rather that loving and obeying God gives us the right perspective and the grace to love our neighbour rightly. Or as Aldous Huxley once put it, trying to love our neighbour without first of all loving God is like trying to take water from a bucket which is never replenished.

The passage describes the character which is necessary for all effective relationships (v2-3). We take it for granted that unselfishness, compassion and sensitive understanding are the essence of the Christian's equipment. Yet maintaining that kind of bearing and those qualities taxes the capacities of many who would consider themselves pillars of the Church. A difference of opinion on a sensitive matter of church policy, or a belief that some new experiment in worship is wrong just because we have grown used to our own pet ways, can unhappily lead to personal recriminations which are totally unjustified. The feeling of this passage has been lost and anger and spite and evil speaking invade the fellowship.

The passage also directs us to the chief end of all our service to God and our neighbour. We are to be a reassurance to them that their lives are not outside the care of God. We are to bring light to the outside world. We cannot be content to be a company of conscientious Christians. We are called to show Christ to the world. That was the task of the Servant of the Lord, the Chosen One, and it is ours.

Questions
1. Is it justifiable to describe the Jews as martyrs to their faith when we look at their modern history?

2. Is it right to say that God has called those devoted teachers, doctors, nurses and so on who have no religious commitment?

3. What evidence of a person's vocation do you consider to be important?

4. A Scots judge recently declared that public opinion was the only possible basis for justice. Do you agree? If not, what other basis is needed?

5. Do you think that such a gentle and self-effacing person as the Servant in this passage could bring justice to the earth?

6. If it is impossible to love our neighbours without first of all loving God, how does that work out in practice?

7. Is suffering always the destiny of the person called to be a prophet?

8. Suggest that the group begin to correspond with a prisoner of conscience.

Chapter 11

The Second Isaiah
(4) The Redeemer of Humankind

His point of view may be summed up in these words; Jahweh is the only God; Israel, his only servant, is entrusted with the task of making him known to all the Gentiles; therefore let the nation of witnesses willingly accept all suffering, for it is assured of triumph in the end.

A. Lods, *The Prophets and the Rise of Judaism*

Passages for study: Isaiah 49:1-8 and 50:4-10

Joy in the Shadows

There is a vivid contrast between these two Servant Songs. Despite one suggestion of discouragement in 49:4, the first is full of assurance and even of joy. The second is shadowed with pain, grief and the darkness of bewilderment and doubt. And there is the suggestion that the two, joy and shadow, are inseparable in the life of the man or woman who is dedicated to the service of God, a remarkable insight for such an early time in human history. The truth is that whatever is creative is always costly. The prophet had perceived that essential fact.

Preachers may find these passages peculiarly helpful because they do highlight elements in the prophet's experience, but they also speak in a more general way to the Church.

The prophet's sense of mission

This sense of mission is very important to our understanding of the background to the life and work of Christ.

Although there is a hostile attitude to Gentiles in much of the Jewish Scriptures, there was also the beginning of a more universal vision. In this passage there is joy in the realisation that the God of Israel will enlighten the whole of humankind.

The book of Jonah, as we shall see, recognises God's concern for Gentiles. And in the Book of Ruth there is the portrait of a Gentile woman of great loyalty and humility, once more a Jewish recognition that Gentiles had a place in the final kingdom of God. So at the time of Christ, that wider vision was not lacking among some Jews, and probably provided a setting for the drama of the growing Church among the Gentiles.

Notice that whereas in the last song (Isaiah 42) the prophet is speaking about the Servant, here it appears to be the Servant himself who is speaking. He has clearly been discouraged, having 'laboured in vain and spent his strength for nought'. Yet even as he is tempted to complain he tells himself that God will be the judge of what he has achieved, and his work is somehow recorded by God himself (v4). It is the kind of assurance that we all need in Christian service, because the final verdict on what we have done must be God's, and not that of ourselves or our fellow workers.

But there is an even greater cause for assurance. His initial task, as that of all the prophets, has been to recall the Israelites (here designated by the name of their ancestor Jacob) to the service of their God (v5). Now he is promised an even greater task. Though only a remnant of Israel return to their loyalty to God, the prophet's word will reach the Gentiles and be a light to them. The prophet will be glorious in the eyes of the Lord who will give him strength (v5-6). We feel here an elation which springs from his confidence in God, and from his sense of being called to this new and supremely important task. It is the high point of hopefulness in the songs.

For a number of reasons in our own day a strong sense of mission tends to be confined to evangelical groups. Other communions have a deep commitment to the service of the needy, the famine-stricken and the oppressed. The compulsion to share the Christian faith with those who do not accept it is less strong.

This is partly because religious belief and moral values have come to be regarded as matters of purely personal concern in which others should not interfere.

This feeling has been accentuated by the presence of devotees of non-Christian religions in our cities and towns. Where there is friendly contact, Christians often discover spiritual riches where they least expect to find them, and develop a great respect for the devotion and thoughtfulness of their Muslim and Buddhist neighbours. So there is born a feeling that to attempt to convert them to Christianity is gravely discourteous.

Perhaps we need to give more considered thought to what Christian mission really means today, in the changed ethnic and social conditions of our time.

The prophet's message and language
In both passages emphasis is laid on the gift of speech and the message of the prophet. In 49:2 the prophet feels that he has a gift of speech like a sharp sword. In 50:4 he is conscious that his mind has been equipped with a message for the weary. The message is renewed day by day, as indeed it must be for the Christian preacher.

There is also an emphasis on listening. Without an open ear there can be no effective witness by prophet or preacher. We may read in a disciplined way, we may share our thoughts profitably in fellowship, and we may learn to present our message cogently. Yet what we are bound to proclaim is more than our own intensely held convictions, more than the declared teaching of the Church. It is all these things tempered by the compelling word which comes to us when, in our prayers, we listen. It is the word for that moment, perhaps never to be repeated or perhaps a permanent new direction to preaching. But it belongs only to whose who cultivate the art of listening, which is just as important as the art of speaking.

The prophet and the redeemer

The prophet is very conscious of the presence of his Lord in the face of the mammoth task to which God has committed him. And the use of the word 'redeemer' here is very important.

As we saw in our study of Jeremiah the 'go'el' or redeemer played a very important part in delivering relatives from debt and slavery and securing justice when they had been killed or injured. This custom helps us to penetrate a little further into the meaning of a word commonly used both in Judaism and Christianity.

If the man had no kin then, in theory, it was the duty of the king to be the go'el or redeemer. The Jews also believed that God himself would act on behalf of those who were ill-used or without human help. He was the great go'el, the great redeemer. This belief crops up in other places in the work of the Second Isaiah, where the prophet declares that God will deliver his people from slavery (43:14, 45:1, 45:13, 52:3).

In this passage, however, the redeemer is concerned for the prophet. He is alone and without help, without friends, despised, the enemy of the people.

The redeemer will ensure that he is heard, that kings and princes heed his message and come to worship the God who is his own preserver.

The message of chapter 42 is repeated in 49:8. The servant will by his life, his message and his persistence be a 'covenant', a promise to the people that God will deliver them.

Verse 9 may imply that the prophet is charged with encouraging the remnant of the people who are still loyal to God to come out of hiding, because they will be safe in the care of their God. It is a passage full of encouragement.

The word 'redeemer' constantly occurs in our hymns, and Paul's Letters in particular frequently allude to the idea of redemption. It is not difficult to see why. The go'el is responsible for paying the price that will secure the land which would be lost, or save the debtor from slavery. It is this last practice which underlies the New Testament idea of redemption. Christ by his death bears the cost of delivering us from the slavery of sin. For instance, in Galatians 3:13 Paul speaks of Christ redeeming Christians from the curse of the law. Again in Ephesians 1:7 we read that in Christ we 'have redemption through his blood, the forgiveness of our trespasses, according to the riches of his grace'.

Some Christians today wish to avoid this kind of language in speaking of Christ's death and resurrection. The idea that Christ pays the price of human sin is repugnant to them. But it is impossible to understand what Christ meant to the early Church without seeing that Paul and others carried over into Christian thinking the figure of God as redeemer from the Old Testament, and applied it to what they believed Christ had done for them. This was no theory. They knew themselves forgiven. They knew a greater moral freedom than they had ever known before. They were at peace with their own conscience. They knew it to be a deliverance and they associated it with the love of Christ offered for them on the cross. There may be better ways of expressing the wonder of that experience. There can be no doubt about the wonder.

The suffering prophet
By contrast with chapter 49, chapter 50 is shadowed. In verse 5 it is clear that the servant has obeyed his God. He is not rebellious. But the people have turned on him and he has been compelled to accept beatings and torture. The servant is finally rejected, and we are prepared for the poetic portrait of the martyr in Isaiah 53.

The amazing fact is that his faith is unimpaired. There is a desperate determination in v7-9. He is still holding to the promise which he had received in 49:7-9, and believes that if he sets himself like flint he will not fail in his faith or witness. He challenges those who will condemn him, openly calling them to state their case (v8). For his own part he puts his trust in God, believing that those who oppose him will wither and die. It is the kind of faith that accounts for the capacity of the Jewish people to survive long centuries of persecution. Nor is it surprising that the early Christians too found in this servant prophet a pattern for the sufferings of Christ.

A message for a crisis
The chapter closes with some words to those who have heeded the prophet's words, and who may well be shaken

and unnerved by what is happening to him, as indeed the disciples of Jesus were in the darkness of Good Friday. They are those who have believed in him, but now walk in darkness and have no light. They are those who have heard a promise from God which, as far as they can see, has not been fulfilled.

We do not expect that those who heed their obedience to God and believe his promises will 'walk in darkness and have no light'. Surely our obedience guarantees us light. Few Christians in Britain today, however, have the experience of oppression and persecution, of being isolated from other Christians, of being deprived of corporate worship, and probably of the Bible and of those aids to devotion which are readily at hand in our homes. We are not threatened. But we have to remember that there are those who, for these very reasons, do walk in darkness and have no light. We can but pray for them and add our voice to such pleas as may be possible for their relief.

The prophet offers his own counsel in 50:10: 'Trust in the name of the Lord.' That phrase 'the name of the Lord' means the authority, power and nature of God as it has been revealed to us. So when it seems that no answer comes to us when we pray, and we have no sense of the presence of God with us in the darkness of doubt and fear, we can but turn and seek to remember what God has shown to us of himself, the very nature which he has revealed to us. As Charles Wesley expressed it as he addressed God, 'Thy nature and thy name is love.' To dwell on what we have seen of God in Jesus and, in the lonely darkness, trust that it is true, even when we have no evidence, may carry us through into the light. It may enable us to heed the other counsel of the prophet – to lean upon God.

There is a prayer which perhaps is fitting for all who, from whatever inward conflict or outward circumstances, find themselves walking in darkness without light:

> Have mercy upon us, O God, in those hours when the world seems empty of thy presence, and no word comes to us from thee; that in the darkness we may wait patiently for the light, and in the silence listen for thy voice, and in all things trust thy promises in Jesus Christ our Lord.

The servant prophet would have understood the spirit of that prayer.

Questions

1. It has been suggested that we are very hazy about the mission of the Church today. How would you define it?
   a) as maintaining the beliefs of the Bible in the world today?
   b) as the moral teacher of the community?
   c) as an evangelical community?
   d) as a channel of Christian love in the world?

2. In practical terms what do you consider to be the mission of your local church?

3. Share any experience where disciplined listening for God whilst you were praying has been answered.

4. What place should the following have in a good sermon?
   a) the beliefs of the Church?
   b) interpretation of biblical passages?
   c) personal convictions?
   d) a call to listeners for a verdict?

5. Try to find contemporary language and ideas which can describe the belief that Christ died to redeem us from the slavery of sin. Do any of our modern hymns help?

6. In addition to persecution, what other experiences may leave Christians in darkness? Do the prophet's words help?

7. Ask each member of the group to bring a prayer which has helped them in spiritual darkness.

Chapter 12

The Second Isaiah
(5) God and the Suffering Servant

All along the history of the world the Sufferer has been the astonishment and stumbling block of humanity. The barbarian gets rid of him; his is the first difficulty with which any young literature wrestles; to the end he remains the problem of philosophy and the sore test of faith. It is not native to men to see meaning or profit in the Sufferer; they are staggered by him; they see no reason or promise in him.

G. Adam Smith, *The Book of Isaiah XL-LXVI*

Passage for study: Isaiah 52:13-15 and 53:1-12

An act of contrition
It is very difficult to dissociate this passage from the figure of Jesus at the time of his Passion. Our earliest acquaintance with the words reflects our faith in the work of Christ on the cross.

Yet to acquire its true value we need to study it in its initial significance. That means we have to understand it as in some way an act of contrition and penitence as well as a confession of hope in God on the part of a Jewish prophet. It also represents the culmination of the Servant's grief and pain. In 49:7 there is a hint that the Servant is meeting hostility, and that people think that he is an enemy of the people. That is confirmed in 50:5-9. Now the blow has fallen and his suffering life has been taken by the oppressors.

The prophet clearly connects the suffering of the Servant with the sins of himself and his people. So here he expresses the penitence of those who have grasped just what his suffering and death mean. Whether the writer speaks simply for himself or for others is uncertain but the penitence is very real.

There is penitence first of all for their failure to penetrate beyond outside appearances. The Servant was unattractive in his weakness and sickness. 'So marred was his appearance, beyond human semblance, and his form beyond that of mortals' (52:14). 'He had no form or majesty that we should look at him, nothing in his appearance that we should desire him' (53:2). So he was rejected and despised.

As Adam Smith has emphasised in the passage which heads this study, men and women do not readily respond to the Sufferer with understanding. They may take pity on him, and go to his assistance in their compassion, but they do not find him in any way attractive. Their assistance is given despite a natural repulsion. To find God speaking to us through a suffering person needs insight and sensitivity that goes beyond pity and compassion, and sometimes requires penitence on our part.

We may, for instance, be genuinely sorry for the victims of pollution or nuclear contamination, but unless we are able to recognise our part as citizens in creating the pollution and indirectly profiting from the power generated by nuclear energy, we are unlikely to make our pity a creative force beyond charitable aid where it is needed. The Suffering Servant calls for penitence. So does the suffering of our day.

The perception of faith
Penitence here is wedded to perception. In 53:4-6 the penitent writer shows an insight more profound than is

reached elsewhere in the Old Testament. The earliest judgement which humanity passes on grief and pain is to ascribe it to wrongdoing. The Sufferer is being punished. The observer looks on with a greater or lesser degree of conscious moral superiority and speculates on the nature of the Sufferer's offence.

The prophet sees the situation entirely differently. The Servant's suffering is vicarious – that is, it is for the sake of other people. He is bearing the griefs of others, including those of the prophet. He has been wounded by their sins. He has paid the cost of their inner peace and his punishment is the means of their healing (53:4-5).

How could the prophet and his fellow penitents come by such knowledge? Only because they have found their own consciences disturbed by the spectacle of the suffering of the Servant. At first they are both repelled and puzzled. Then, as they seek an explanation, they feel a burden of guilt because they have treated him so badly. They recognise that, far from being a man deserving punishment, he is one whose suffering is totally undeserved. The contrast between what they recognise in him and what they know of themselves covers them with shame. And then, inexplicably, in the remembrance of his goodness they find peace and healing.

Adam Smith suggests that here the prophet teaches us that vicarious suffering is not a dogmatic but an experimental truth.

Perhaps that is the key to our understanding of Christian belief. The relationship between Christ's suffering and our redemption remains theoretical and somehow unreal until it is perceived in experience. The disturbed conscience, the recognised contrast between Christ's goodness and our own twisted natures, the decision to take him at his word and to live by God's forgiveness are steps in that journey of experience which translates a doctrine into faith.

The bearing of the servant

It is very difficult to read verses 7-9 without remembering the Passion of Christ, the parallel is so close. But the circumstances appear to be different.

Adam Smith has pointed out that in the Old Testament and especially in the Psalms the two outstanding misfortunes of a person's life were sickness and the miscarriage of justice. Both are represented in this passage but in verses 7-9 it is the failure of justice which we contemplate.

His death has all the appearance of a misuse of the processes of the law. Adam Smith translates verse 8:

> By tyranny and law was he taken;
> And of his age who reflected,
> That he was wrenched from the land of the living.

This is the kind of process only too familiar in our century when show trials were both the public theatre and the threatening display of state power which kept whole nations cowed. The individual, however innocent, however just, is easily crushed by the juggernaut which can manipulate the institutions of justice. The plight of the Servant bids us beware.

Jesus was crucified not by an over-powerful state, but as the result of pressure placed on a pliable state official by intolerant and offended religious leaders. But the bearing of both Christ and the Servant was the same. They bore suffering without complaint (v7). They were honest and guiltless of any wrong doing (v9).

The first part of verse 9 is rather difficult. That he was put to death as a criminal is clear. But both Adam Smith and Moffat think that the Authorised Version is a mistranslation of the next phrase which should read 'they buried him with felons' not with 'the rich'. This makes the undeserved shame the more repellent.

The purpose of God

With verse 10 we reach the most difficult part of the chapter. Suddenly we are faced with a different explanation. Until now we have been led to believe that the Servant's death is the responsibility of powerful, unjust and sinful men whom no one dare oppose. Now we are told that this was the purpose of God. It was God who bruised him and laid sickness upon him and allowed him to be put to death unjustly. This raises two issues.

The first is contained in the words 'when you make his life an offering for sin'. Here the prophet has chosen to interpret the Servant's death in sacrificial terms.

Both in the Pentateuch and in the prophecy of Ezekiel provision is made for reparation for wrongdoing. In Numbers 5:7-8 there is a payment to the person who has been wronged. In Leviticus (5:14-16 and 6:1-7) there is a sacrifice to be made over and above compensation to the wronged party. By this sacrifice a priest made atonement for the breaking of the law and the wrongdoer was pardoned.

Clearly the prophet wants us to understand that a human life rather than that of an animal has been sacrificed. It is impossible to say just what prompted this assertion. There are signs in the Old Testament that the sacrificial system did not always satisfy the most sensitive spirits. Hosea claims that God wants love and compassion rather than sacrifice, and Psalm 51:16-17 claims:

> For you have no delight in sacrifice; if I were to give a burnt offering, you would not be pleased. The sacrifice acceptable to God is a broken spirit; a broken and contrite heart, O God, you will not despise.

Both Hosea and the Psalms leave the sacrificial system well behind, claiming that penitence and love are what God requires of us. Our prophet tries to make the idea of sacrifice in atonement for sin work in a new way, through the death of a good man. Christianity inherited the thought of Hosea, the psalmist and Second Isaiah. But it is the latter whose thought undoubtedly influenced the early Church and especially Paul. It is the apostle who speaks of Jesus' death as an offering for sin.

In the second place these verses raise a problem for many Christians. The idea that God would actually will the suffering of a good man they find repulsive and unacceptable. If God genuinely loves his children then he would surely not inflict any injury upon them. If there is injury it must be the result of human sin.

Yet it is surprising how often some great Christians feel that God has visited them with affliction. John Woolman, the 18th century American Quaker, speaks of God visiting him with a serious illness in order to reclaim him for a true Christian life. The anonymous author of the medieval *The Cloud of Unknowing* suggests that God takes away our joy in order to test our patience and so enable us to grow as Christians. And although God is never mentioned, Oscar Wilde has a penetrating comment on sorrow:

It seems to me that Love of some kind is the only possible explanation of the extraordinary amount of suffering that there is in the world. I cannot conceive any other explanation . . . If the worlds have been built out of sorrow it has been by the hands of love, because in no other way could the soul of man . . . reach the full stature of its perfection.

It is a humbling comment.

The prophet is right to believe that where there is suffering God can never be far away, and where that suffering is innocent suffering that, indeed, God is very near. What we would say is that God does not allow suffering to run to waste, that because he is so close to the Suffering Servant his transforming grace enables that suffering to have a positive outcome. Men and women are moved to penitence, as the early verses of the chapter show, and in their penitence and faith they find peace.

The Servant is content
T. T. Robinson, commenting on these closing verses, has noticed a remarkable insight in verse 11. We ask petulantly where is the justice in allowing the innocent to suffer for the guilty. But the passage suggests that the Servant is actually satisfied. That seems almost impossible to us but let Robinson speak for himself:

There are moments of vision, when the immediate outlook is at its blackest, in which a sense of the truth comes home to him, and he knows. With that perfect self-surrender which is the primary condition of his service, he can look out over the years and see the line of those who are in the deepest spiritual sense his children, with whom he has travailed, and for whom his pain has won life. And with this insight into the eternal reality his own problem and his discontent disappear. He suffers, but they live and in their life he finds his own.

Is it true? Only the sufferer in those circumstances can tell us. We know it can happen where men and women sacrifice themselves to save lives. I remember hearing the moving story of an African chieftain who insisted on being brought to a London hospital, where he died in terrible loneliness and weakness, fortified by the hope that medical research into his disease – sleeping sickness – might save the lives of future members of his tribe. And he was content.

It is also possible that men and women who spend their lives in the service of inadequate or at least potentially criminal characters must find what contentment they can in something very akin to the experience Robinson has described. Almost daily they must be disappointed and discouraged, and badly let down by untrustworthy, weak-willed, or deliberately destructive and self-centred clients. Unless they are to become cynical and allow their sights to fall they must find their contentment in the limited achievement which they see, but with the undying hope that they have laboured to a greater effectiveness than is visible. And some very serene social workers, probation officers and prison chaplains suggest by their serenity that this may well be the case.

The concluding sentence of this picture of the Servant also completes our understanding of the meaning of vicarious suffering. It tells us something of both the resource which makes it possible and the expression of love which makes it effective. From his place among the transgressors (v12) the Servant prays for the felons around him. He is so close to God that he knows that only God's grace can redeem their lives, and he is close enough to know that 'the love of God is broader than the measure of man's mind' and that his prayers will be heard.

As we contemplate with increasing anxiety the incidence of crime, especially among youngsters, I wonder if it ever occurs to us that if we prayed for them God would hear our prayers and answer.

Questions

1. Comment on the words of Adam Smith concerning the Sufferer. Do you consider that he is accurate in his observation?

2. Considerable suffering is caused by social selfishness, on all our parts. Is social penitence the key to reform?

3. Soon after the accession of Hitler, Dietrich Bonhoeffer said that the Church should put a spoke in the wheel of a government which persecuted Jews. What responsibility has the Church where there is manifest injustice?

4. 'The Passion of Christ is only comprehensible to those who have experienced its grace.' Discuss.

5. Look carefully at these two contrasting views and discuss their truthfulness:

   'Pain is the blessed means of God' and
   'It is blasphemous to impute to God a desire to cause suffering.'

6. 'God does not intend us to be happy. He intends us to love.' Do you agree?

7. Is it possible to believe that a person might be content to suffer quite innocently if he believed that his suffering had given a new moral freedom to others?

Chapter 13

Jonah
God and the need of the world

The world is my parish.

John Wesley

Passage for study: The book of Jonah.

A controversial book
There are few books in the Bible which have been so differently interpreted as the book of Jonah.

Many commentators have concentrated their attention on the episode in which Jonah was swallowed by the whale – or the great fish, as the text says. This has been interpreted as a 'type', predicting the three days between the crucifixion and the resurrection.

Other scholars have believed that the story is a kind of parable teaching a particular lesson about the ways of God. This interpretation has been met with indignation by more conservative Christians. In fact a sermon on Jonah has always been likely to offend one or other section of a congregation.

Perhaps in the end it does not matter whether we treat it as a folk-tale, a parable or a rather marvellous historical happening, as long as we recognise that it carries a deeply challenging truth, not only for the time of Jonah but for all time.

The background
We shall only understand the story if we understand the background.

The book belongs to the age after the Exile when the Jews had painfully, and amid much discouragement, rebuilt Jerusalem and were seeking to rebuild also the religious life of the people. The books of Ezra and Nehemiah tell this story.

Both these books assume that Jerusalem had been punished by God because the people had mixed with other nations, not only mingling with them in trade, but intermarrying. Ezra 9:10f makes this clear. The verses embody a prayer acknowledging this sin:

> And now, O God, what shall we say after this? For we have forsaken your commandments, which you commanded by your servants the prophets, saying, 'The land that you are entering to possess is a land unclean with the pollutions of the peoples of the lands, with their abominations ... Therefore do not give your daughters to their sons, neither take their daughters for your sons, and never seek their place or prosperity, so that you may be strong and eat the good of the land and leave it for an inheritance to your children forever.'

So it is recorded in Ezra 10 that all who have intermarried with other races were compelled to put away their wives. And in the last chapter of Nehemiah (13:23f) the prohibition is repeated and separation once more ordered.

Thus there arose a racial attitude very little different from 20th century apartheid, the surrounding peoples regarded as inferior as well as hostile. This was reinforced by much of the later Old Testament literature. Despite the earlier warnings of prophets like Amos and the exhortations of the Second Isaiah, the Jews looked forward to the Day of the Lord as a day when their enemies would be routed and punished, and when they would rule the world in the name of their God. It is against that background that the Book of Jonah, and also the Book of Ruth, are to be seen. Both plead for a greater understanding of God's purpose for the peoples of the earth and a greater insight into the lives of those whom they regard as their enemies.

The true vocation of Israel

You may remember that in Isaiah 49:6 the Servant had been instructed about his true vocation. He was not simply to gather Israel, the people of God, back to their true loyalty, but 'as a light to the nations, that my salvation may reach to the end of the earth'. The same sentiment, probably based on the words of Isaiah, is to be found in Luke 2:32, in the words of the Nunc Dimittis. Simeon speaks of having seen God's salvation, 'a light to lighten the Gentiles and the glory of thy people Israel'.

It is that vocation which the writer of the book of Jonah believes Israel is refusing to accept. In 1:2 the call is clear. Jonah is to go to preach in Gentile Nineveh, and he flees in the opposite direction to avoid such a task.

By the time this story was written Nineveh was of course no longer a great city, capital of a conquering people. It had once been a city notorious for its profligacy and immoral living, and here it is used symbolically to show that even the most notorious of evil cities must hear the message of God.

The next part of the story is typical of the Old Testament in that it emphasises that God is not so easily thwarted by human disobedience. The ship on which Jonah is sailing is caught in a storm. The writer without hesitation attributes this to the determination of God that Jonah shall do his duty (v4). The crew also see the hand of God in the storm, and are convinced that they have on board a guilty person because of whom all their lives are being jeopardised. So they draw lots (v8-10) to find a solution.

The drawing of lots has always been seen as a way of discovering the will of God among unsophisticated peoples. It was used by the apostles in the New Testament in order to fill the place vacated by Judas Iscariot. In a trial it was sometimes used on the assumption that through lots God would expose the culprit. The principle is not unlike that common in the Middle Ages where if a witness made a mistake in the words of the oath it was assumed that God was exposing him as a perjured witness. Readers of George Eliot's novels may remember that she refers to Methodists still using lots when describing the Methodists in *Adam Bede,* and shows how Silas Marner was the victim of trickery in the chapel when he was wrongly convicted of theft by the use of lots.

The obedience of Jonah, once his guilt is exposed, and his readiness to sacrifice himself to save the crew of the ship, is in vivid contrast to his original flight. Perhaps this is intended to suggest that, despite their unreadiness to accept their true vocation, the Jews were upright, conscientious and generally unselfish people, quite capable of self-sacrifice for the sake of others. They were simply blind to the purpose of God in this direction.

An interpolation
Chapter 2 is an interpolation. From the belly of the great fish Jonah is depicted as praying to God. The words are fairly obviously a psalm. To find psalms used in this way as prayers is not uncommon in the later prophets. Notice, for instance, two prayers in Jeremiah 17:7-8 and 12-14 which we have already commented upon. And Isaiah 12 belongs to the same category. In Jonah the original writer seems to

be describing an experience of intense suffering from which he has already been delivered, rather than praying for deliverance (v2 and 7). Physical metaphors are used to express spiritual agonies and the depth of the experience is stressed in v3, 5 and 6. Some scholars think that the book originally went straight from 2:1 to 2:10, and that this misplaced psalm has been added later for effect. It certainly adds nothing to the theme.

A penitent people

The description of Nineveh as so great that it would take three days to pass through it is obviously hyperbole. But it conveys the sense of a great people receiving Jonah's message from God.

The immediate response of the king and people seems almost unbelievable. Few Christian evangelists in any century have had quite so electric an effect. Perhaps the writer had it in mind to draw a contrast between the tardy responses of the Israelites to the prophets and the readiness of these despised Gentiles to turn to God in penitence. One is reminded of the gospel story of the centurion's servant in Luke 7 where Jesus emphasises the contrast between the suspicion and lack of faith which he was meeting among his own people and the remarkable faith of the Gentile centurion. Doubtless readers of Jonah in his day might have reacted with the same indignation as some of Jesus' own hearers would have done to such a comment.

The readiness of God to pardon Nineveh reiterates the message of the book which is to show that God is merciful to all who are penitent, regardless of race.

A sulky preacher

Chapter 4 is the key chapter of the whole book. Here immediately the anger of Jonah reflects what the writer knows of the unreadiness of the Jews to believe that God could be as gracious and merciful to Gentiles as to his own people.

The initial verses (4:1-3) are reminiscent of Elijah despairing of his task in recalling Israel back to God. He was ready to die because he had been so ineffective. Here, however, Jonah wants to die because his preaching has succeeded. There may well be irony in the writer's mind. That Jonah knows in his heart that God will be merciful also suggests that the writer believes that his people are deliberately closing their minds to what their consciences know to be true. Not an uncommon fault, even among Christians!

The little story about the gourd, or bush, (4:5-9) is a parable. The shelter which it gives to Jonah as he sits in the sun and in the searing wind arouses his gratitude and when the gourd withers and he is left without shelter he despairs for himself but also feels sorry for the gourd. In 4:9-11 the point of the parable is drawn out in the words of God to Jonah. If Jonah had pity on the gourd, should not God himself have pity on the teeming thousands of people in Nineveh and even on their cattle?

The last verse must be one of the most moving verses in the Old Testament. It suggests that here was a writer who like the Second Isaiah has come to know God as 'gracious and merciful, slow to anger and of great kindness' (4:2) and that he is able to rejoice in the knowledge that that great love embraces not only his own people but the whole of the human race. There is compassion here as well as a freedom from all racial exclusiveness. The lonely voice of the writer of the book of Jonah can be heard in vivid contrast to much else in the Old Testament, and heralds a day when Christian preachers would carry that same message to a waiting world.

Some reflections

The story belongs to its own age. The absolute control of God over the elements was taken for granted. Today such an interference would not be expected by most faithful Christians. Nor would we assume that drawing lots would somehow give God a chance to choose a suitable servant or expose a culprit. God gives human beings the intellect to make decisions and arrive at verdicts. Sometimes human frailty may impair the judgement. But where intelligence is used with humility, then God's will surely can be realised without recourse to the irrational.

Most of us today would claim to be colour-blind, and few Christians surely would be happy to support racist policies. Yet it is possible to slip into attitudes which are in conflict with our Christian profession. In towns and cities where Christians rub shoulders with people from other ethnic groups, they do not always understand their ways and in irritation may make snap judgements which place an increasing distance between them and their neighbours. Perhaps too we are not always ready to protest at unfairness and intimidation against ethnic minorities. This may be as much our true vocation as Christians as the visit to Nineveh was for Jonah, or the outstretched hand of friendship to Gentiles was for Jews.

Our story emphasises the nature of God's mercy and love. A number of times in these studies we have chosen to emphasise the fact that in God's moral order deeds have consequences. The message of Jonah and of our own gospel is that where men and women recognise that moral order and acknowledge their own failures and folly, the mercy and love of God have no limits – for ourselves and for those we so often fail to understand and, even more desperately, fail to love.

Questions
1. We are appointing a new circuit steward. What are the fors and againsts of drawing lots?

2. Remembering the recent history of apartheid, could Israel in those distant centuries be blamed for racism as exemplified in the books of Ezra and Nehemiah?

3. The old Covenant Service contains two prayers asking pardon
   a) wherein we have been thoughtless in our judgements, hasty in condemnation, grudging in forgiveness.
   b) if we have been eager for the punishment of wrongdoers and slow to seek their redemption.

   Discuss these prayers in the light of the book of Jonah.

4. When a person who has committed a serious offence professes penitence even Christians are apt to be suspicious and not always ready to meet that penitence with generosity and support. Look at the issues that are involved.

5. How important is it in these increasingly intolerant days for Christians to give strong support to all movements promoting a) racial harmony b) deeper understanding between the Christian Church and other faiths?

6. Does it really matter whether the story of Jonah is a fiction with a moral, or a historical fact?

7. Write some prayers suitable for a service on Social Responsibility Sunday with special reference to race relations.

Epilogue
Between the old and the new

In the minds of all of us a few great affirmations contend with doubts and speculations as widening experience puts them to the test. The Old Testament sets this process before us on the large scale of history and bears impressive witness that through all the uncertainties faith advances towards something surer and finer . . . Nevertheless to see clearly whither the process is tending we must look beyond the Old Testament to the New.

C. H. Dodd, *The Authority of the Bible*

Summing it up

This epilogue is designed to sum up the discoveries unearthed by our studies, and in the process to show how the Old Testament still leaves us with questions which are cannot be resolved within the context of the Jewish faith. This is what Dodd is saying in the quotation which heads our epilogue. In seeking to deal with this we shall put the Old Testament in its true context within the Christian faith as the experience of the Hebrews, their reflections upon that experience, and our conviction that God spoke through their prophets as a prelude to the word he spoke through his Son.

The problem of the vocation of Israel

We pick up the first great problem at the point where we ended our last study. How is it possible to reconcile the consciousness of Israel's special relationship with God, their status as a chosen and peculiar people with the belief expressed in the book of Jonah that Gentiles are equally loved by God?

The prophets take the special relationship for granted.

For Hosea the relationship with God is close and his concern is that it should not be broken. The wider scene only impinged on his thought because disaster was likely to ensue from military defeat by foreign enemies.

Amos recognised that all the nations had a responsibility to God, but his words were a judgement on everyone.

Isaiah of Jerusalem was concerned like Hosea for the holiness of his own people, and very anxious that Israel should stand aloof from other peoples, lest their religious beliefs and practices contaminated those of God's people.

Jeremiah was deeply aware of the impending fall of Jerusalem and of the isolation which his message entailed. Like Amos he pronounced judgement against other nations, but his message of hope seems to be confined to his own people.

It is the Second Isaiah and the writer of the book of Jonah whose vision carried them to the point where they could see the true vocation of Israel as a light to the Gentiles. The genius for religion which characterised the Jews was a gift of God, but, for these writers, it was not a privilege conveying conscious superiority. Rather it laid upon them a responsibility to bring other peoples to know their God.

The collision between this message and the tradition we noticed in the books of Ezra and Nehemiah still existed in the days of Jesus. Gentiles had become Jews by religious faith, but only by accepting circumcision and the edicts of the Jewish Law in all its intricate detail. It was left to Paul to preach a gospel that went beyond the Law. As Paul wrote, the Law had been a schoolmaster to bring men to Christ. The gospel of grace could break down barriers, reconciling people of all nations to Christ and to each other.

The problem of sin

How sinful people can approach a holy God has always been a problem for religion. As we have seen, it was Micah who articulated the problem: 'With what shall I come before the Lord, and bow myself before God on high?' (Micah 6:6).

Like Micah, Hosea and Amos showed little enthusiasm for the system of sacrifices. Hosea claimed that God wanted compassion rather than burnt offerings and Micah proposed that doing justly, loving mercy and walking humbly with God were the secret of obedience to him. But that leaves two deep-seated problems.

Firstly, there is the problem of guilt. This is not just a formal, theological matter. It is a psychological and profoundly spiritual matter as well. On one side the sacrificial system may have been an attempt to 'win over' a displeased God. It was also designed to ease a conscience which refused to give its owner any peace.

Guilt can be very destructive. It undermines the will and weakens us when we struggle with our own selfishness and faults. It can cripple the conscience so that slowly but inexorably we lose our capacity for sensitive moral judgement and accept that which once we would have rejected as unworthy. It can deprive us of any real hope about the future, and indirectly it can impair our physical health. So forgiveness and moral healing are imperative for healthy, whole lives.

Secondly, being just, compassionate and humble is not a straightforward matter. We are not naturally just. Compassion can sometimes be a momentary emotion when we are moved, say, by the sight of hungry and suffering children. But to sustain compassion may be a different matter. As for being humble, our fat relentless egos are a constant hindrance. So we need grace, and grace abounding.

The Old Testament found no alleviation for that need except through the sacrificial system, though devout and God-fearing individuals like Jeremiah could believe that God would heal them in heart and mind. We shall never know the full extent of the personal religious devotion of the later centuries of Judaism. A glance through the Psalms and some of the non-biblical writings of the centuries immediately before Christ suggests that there was a belief in a divine forgiveness among the Jews which was independent of the sacrificial system. How widespread that belief was it is difficult to say. In any case, as far as the Old Testament was concerned, the nearest approach to a gospel is to be found in Jeremiah 31:33, with the promise that God would write his laws on the hearts of his people. It was on that faith that Jesus built the New Testament gospel.

The problem of transcendence
In Solomon's prayer at the dedication of the Temple (1 Kings 8:27) he said:

> But will God indeed dwell on the earth? Even heaven and the highest heaven cannot contain you, much less this house that I have built!

That sentiment encapsulates the tension which existed in Old Testament religion. The more the people realised that God was not simply a tribal God, their protector and battle winner, but, as Amos shrewdly perceived and the Second Isaiah poetically proclaimed, the God of Creation, the more remote and transcendent he seemed to be. How could the Creator of the ends of the earth dwell with individual people?

The older belief was that God was present in the Law, indeed that in a way God *was* the Law. As long as Israel possessed the Torah God was with them. He was their moral guide and provided the social cement which made them a people.

Later Jewish thinkers, however, were concerned that the presence of God should touch the individual at a deeper level. So Wisdom, which was both the intellectual power of God that devised creation and the spirit that inspired moral attitudes and comprehension of the human mind, became in the centuries leading to the Christian era the expression of the presence of God.

Yet even that was not enough. Simone Weil in a remarkable passage has highlighted our human dilemma:

> The infinity of space and time separates us from God. How are we to seek for him? How are we to go towards him? Even if we were to walk for hundreds of years, we should do no more than go round and round the world . . . We are incapable of progressing vertically. We cannot take a step towards the heavens. God crosses the universe and comes to us.

Here is the secret of the incarnation. The Word became flesh because God crossed the universe and came to us. And on the day when the world crucified the Word, the symbol of that holiness and transcendence which formed a gulf between God and his sinful world, the veil of the Temple, was rent. God not only came to his world, but no religious observance could keep him out. The aspiration of the Old Testament awaited the New.

The problem of suffering

The Old Testament, like human life, is beset by suffering. At first it did not seem a religious problem so much as a purely practical one. How to cope with suffering, with pain, with grief, with death was then, as now, a momentous challenge. But as long as people believed suffering to be a judgement on the sinfulness of the sufferer, no religious question emerged.

The religious question, when it did emerge, was simple enough. Why do the righteous suffer and the wicked prosper? Amos would never have asked that question. Neither would his fellow eighth-century prophets. Jeremiah, on the other hand, had experienced undeserved suffering and occasionally resented it. Yet he could not devise an answer which separated suffering from punishment.

It was the Second Isaiah who produced the most sensitive answer. Suffering could never be other than suffering. No euphemism could disguise its power to distort human life. But the prophet saw, probably in the life of a very great man, that suffering could emancipate and heal other men and women. Suffering could be vicarious, but in the realisation of what his suffering could accomplish, the sufferer might even be content.

It is a mark of the outstanding insight of this poet-prophet that Jesus himself appears to have accepted the model supplied by the Second Isaiah as the pattern for his own life. Luke, in recording the death of Jesus, saw in him the Suffering Servant. The prophet himself could not see so far ahead, but perhaps it was in this momentous question that in his words, the Old Testament came nearest to the New. Without realising it the prophet was describing in human terms suffering which we as Christians believe is at the heart of God.

The problem of hope

By the time of Christ the Jews were very divided about their hope for the future.

Some, following what they took to be prophecies in the book of Daniel, looked forward to the advent of a great military leader, a descendant of David, who would establish once more the great kingdom of the past and expel Israel's conquerors. It was a very nationalistic and political hope.

Others looked for a different kind of Messiah, one who would bring spiritual transformation to the people. It was probably from among such Jews that the early Jewish Christians emerged.

Beyond that, among the Pharisees there was the hope that when the people obeyed the Law with perfect conscientiousness God would establish his kingdom and those who had died would rise again to life to share in the joy of that kingdom.

In the 'Wisdom of Solomon', a book from the Apochrypha, written around the time of Christ, there is a passage which expresses faith in a life beyond death:

> But the righteous live forever, and their reward is with the Lord; the Most High takes care of them. Therefore they will receive a glorious crown and a beautiful diadem from the hand of the Lord, because with his right hand he will cover them, and with his arm he will shield them . . . In the eyes of the foolish they seemed to have died, and their departure was thought to be a disaster, and their going from us to be their destruction; but they are at peace. For though in the sight of others they were punished, their hope is full of immortality.
>
> Wisdom 5:15-16, 3:2-5

Such a personal hope, however, seems to be absent from the Old Testament. Attempts have been made to find some hope of personal immortality in the Psalms and in one passage from Job:

> I know that my Redemmer lives, and that at the last he will stand upon the earth; and after my skin has been thus destroyed, then in my flesh I shall see God.

It may be that the writer is looking for some solution to the problem of suffering which involved a compensation to the sufferer in another life, but it is far from clear what he means. Moreover in another passage he speaks as though death was the end:

> Let me alone, that I may find a little comfort before I go, never to return, to the land of gloom and deep darkness, the land of gloom and chaos, where light is like darkness.
>
> Job 10:20-22

In the light of that statement the previous expression of hope seems unlikely to refer to life after death. One can only conclude that there is no sure sign that a personal hope was part of the later Old Testament faith.

Conclusion
The Christian faith stands on the foundation of the prophetic message. It has inherited the moral concern with an awareness of the holiness of God, so that moral obedience has become the true outcome of the awe and wonder of worship. The gospel proclaims spiritual renewal as Jeremiah did, and rejoices in the good news of God come to people in Christ, with the same joy with which the Second Isaiah proclaimed the deliverance from the Exile. The Church reaches out with the compassion of the book of

Jonah. And the Suffering Servant is brought to birth in Bethlehem. We have the privilege of knowing that God 'who at sundry times and in divers manners spake in times past unto the fathers by the prophets, hath in these last days spoken unto us by his Son'.

Questions

1. The Jews were faced with the task of bringing light to the Gentiles, and recognising that they were also children of God. What is the task of the Church today, to convert people of other faiths, or to learn from them?

2. We have described some of the effects of human guilt. How far does the practice of confession in some Churches seem an advance on general confession in public worship?

3. If we had only the moral law to remind us of the presence of God, what more should we need from our faith?

4. A recent preacher on Radio 4 said that we can only accept suffering and try to make the best of it, leaving the rest to God. Is this adequate or has the Old Testament something more to say?

5. What do you consider to be the most serious problem which the Old Testament left for the New to resolve?

6. Of the prophets you have studied which do you consider to offer you the greatest light on God and our responsibility to him today?

References

Scripture quotations, unless otherwise stated, are from the New Revised Standard Version of the Bible, copyright 1989 by the Division of Christian Education of the National Council of the Churches of Christ in the USA.

Page

3	Francis Thompson, 'The Hound of Heaven'.
7	From J. B. Phillips, *The Four Prophets* (in this case translations of Hosea).
7	J. B. Phillips, op. cit. (translations of Hosea).
12	Trevor Huddleston, *Naught for Your Comfort,* Fontana.
12	J. B. Phillips, op. cit. (translation of Amos).
15	J. B. Phillips, op. cit. (translation of Amos).
18	Henry McKeating, *Studying the Old Testament,* p97, Epworth Press.
19	Conor Cruise O Brien, *The Observer,* June 1983.
22	E. W. Heaton, *The Old Testament Prophets,* p122 Pelican.
22	Colin Morris, *Starting from Scratch*, Epworth Press.
25	*MHB* 531 (not the *H&P* version).
27	Richard Rolle, *The Fire of Love,* p64, Penguin.
29	Simone Weil, *Waiting on God*, p167, Fontana.
31	Evelyn Underhill, *Worship*, p79, Nisbet.
24-26	J. B. Phillips, op. cit. (translation of Micah).
34	Paul Tillich, *The Eternal Now*, p31, SCM.
36	Blaise Pascal, *Pensées*.
39	Robert Browning, *The Ring and the Book*.
41	Oesterley and Robinson, *Hebrew Religion; Its Origin and Development*, p224, SPCK.
45	H. H. Rowley, *The Rediscovery of the Old Testament*, p128, James Clarke.

54	Alice Meynell, quoted by June Badeni in *The Slender Tree*, p75, Tabb House, 1981.
54	Dietrich Bonhoeffer, *Letter and Papers from Prison*, SCM.
54	Simone Weil, *Waiting on God*, p53, Fontana.
58	Julian of Norwich, *Revelations of Divine Love*, p109, Penguin.
61	*MHB* 910.
62	Dietrich Bonhoeffer, op. cit.
68	H. H. Farmer, *The World and God*, p92, Nisbet.
74	H. H. Farmer, op. cit. p95.
77	Kenneth Clark, *Civilisation*, BBC.
78	Henry Vaughan, 'The World'.
80	Nicholai Berdyaev, *The Meaning of History*, p116, G. Bles.
86	H. H. Rowley, op. cit. p60.
88	T. H. Robinson, *Prophecy and the Prophets in Ancient Israel*, p170, Duckworth.
96	A. Lods, *The Prophets and the Rise of Judaism*, p248, Routledge.
103	From *New Every Morning*, BBC.
105 & 108	G. Adam Smith, *The Book of Isaiah vol. 2*, p347, Hodder.
111	Oscar Wilde, 'De Profundis' *Works*, p921.
111	T. H. Robinson, op. cit. p173.
122	C. H. Dodd, *The Authority of the Bible*, p190, Nisbet.
126	Simone Weil, op. cit. p167.